THE
LITTLE
HISTORY
OF
THE EAST END

THE
LITTLE
HISTORY
OF
THE EAST END

DEE GORDON

First published 2020

The History Press
97 St George's Place, Cheltenham,
Gloucestershire, GL50 3QB
www.thehistorypress.co.uk
© Dee Gordon, 2020

British Library Cataloguing in Publication Data.
A catalogue record for this book is available from the British
Library.

ISBN 978 0 7509 9196 4

Typesetting and origination by The History Press
Printed in Turkey by Imak.

MIX
Paper from
responsible sources
FSC
www.fsc.org   FSC® C013056

CONTENTS

This book is dedicated to the best East End parents ever,
George and Dora Winston

INTRODUCTION

This has been a fascinating book to research. Although I was born and brought up in Whitechapel, and have written a couple of books about the East End, not to mention reading many on the subject, I thought I was well acquainted with the area's history. Not so! On this journey, I have learned such a lot about the area, its people, its shifting status, its highs and its lows. My affection for my roots is undaunted, and it is this affection I hope to share, from the East End's embryonic beginnings to its twenty-first-century façade – and it is indeed a façade, for it is necessary to dig deep to find the true nature of the place.

I hope you will love learning about it as much as I did. You will notice that I have only touched on some of its more famous 'stories' – Jack the Ripper and the Krays for instance. This is for two reasons: the East End has a light side to offset the dark side, and there are a huge number of books and websites dedicated to such specific parts of its history. As you will see, the East End has a lot more to offer than criminals and, in a 'Little History' with its suggested limitations, the main focus is on local growth and change with just a nod to its elaborate and extensive political and religious history. It could have otherwise proved to be quite a daunting read, and that is not the intention. Apologies if I have left out your favourite bit of East End history!

To clarify, 'my' East End is bounded by the River Thames in the south, the River Lea in the east, the City of London in the west and Victoria Park on the Hackney border in the north. This represents postcodes E1, E2, E3 and – though it may sound odd, but I didn't choose the postcodes! – E14.

ACKNOWLEDGEMENTS

I am particularly indebted to the staff at the Tower Hamlets Local History Archive in Stepney, although the staff at the Museum of London, the British Library and the Museum of Docklands, as well as Dan Heather at the Royal London Hospital Archive, have also proved very helpful. Lesley Love and her Facebook community (East London Days Gone By) offered help, especially with images, as have some of the Flickr community especially Hornbeam Arts, Maggie Jones, Rob Higgins, Simon Harriyott, Richard Nevell and Tom Bastin. Images have been gratefully sourced via Wellcome Images, the Institute of Historical Research, the National Brewery Heritage Trust, the National Brewery Centre, Dr Neil Clifton, Neil Powell (battlefieldhistorian.com) and Robert Wynn Jones (lostcityoflondon.co.uk) in addition to more traditional sources. All copyright sources have been investigated and checked, apart from the anonymous postcards belonging to the author's own collection. I would also like to thank Nicola Guy and the staff at The History Press in Gloucestershire; a long way from the East End, but with some empathy for the subject regardless.

Woolly mammoth. *Bulletin of the Geological Society of America, 1890*

1

FROM THE STONE AGE TO THE ROMANS

THE FIRST COCKNEYS?

No Bow Bells so no Cockneys, but a few early Ice Age wanderers as much as a million years ago were likely to have been travelling across what we now call Europe, from the African continent, with no North Sea to cross. Could pre-Neanderthals (*homo erectus*) have been hunting lions, bears, rhinos and even elephants in the area now known as the East End of London? Or did hunting only gather pace with the advent of woolly mammoths, reindeer and horses? Such animals would perhaps have been driven into the marshes in that vicinity to make them 'easier' to catch. Foraging for nuts and fruit would have added to a carnivorous diet. There are no confirmed signs of 'human' life, however, in and around London until after 110,000 BC, even though tools made by an early species of human were found less than 100 miles away, in Suffolk, from over half a million years ago.

The River Thames is thought to have been on its current course for half a million years, its formation and route dictated by ice sheets. The Lea Valley was formed, similarly, by flooding spreading southward as a result of glacial melt as late as *c.* 10,000 BC but was believed to be populated (if scantily) soon after. As the North Sea plains flooded, the resultant river valleys meant that early hunter-gatherers could pass through what is likely to have been dense forest, and the Thames would have been one of those rivers forced into a new route. Climate warming meant that the levels of the River Thames and River Lea rose over the next few thousand years, and the local landscape slowly changed, becoming more fertile around what is now Stepney, Bow and Bethnal Green. (Note the use of the popular spelling Lea rather than the often used Lee, to avoid confusion.) The Thames itself is now a shadow of its former, early self.

Historians certainly argue for the presence of early hunter-gatherers in the area from around 4000 BC, bearing in mind that various species of humans virtually disappeared with every recurrent Ice Age (every 100,000 years or so). The earliest skeleton found in the area covered by this book dates from as early as 3900 BC. This was found in Blackwall and, interestingly, was revealed to be in the foetal position – which could indicate either a ritual return to Mother Earth, or some need for a small grave. Early humans, as in other parts of early Britain, would have lived by hunting on the then marshy areas on the banks of rivers such as the Thames, the latter becoming more of a farming community once they started growing additional food around 3500 BC. Wheat grains were found in the Canning Town area which were dated to *c.* 3000 BC. Early finds of stone tools and weapons in the Thames Valley date from this period, then bronze finds followed by iron implements from around 800 BC (hence Stone, Bronze and Iron Ages, of course). Excavations in nearby Hackney Brook revealed a plethora of tools dating from *c.* 4000 BC – the same area where the bones of woolly mammoths, and even a crocodile, pre-date modern humans.

A PLACE TO CALL 'OME SWEET 'OME

There was a prehistoric mound, known as Friars Mount, which some historians have regarded as being where Arnold Circus in Shoreditch is now, a suitable location for early dry and defensible settlement, although its specific origins are virtually impossible to date. What is a little easier to establish is that this area was the site of one of the principal springs of the now subterranean Walbrook River, one of over twenty tributaries of the Thames. Its swampy banks (i.e. Shoreditch), along with those of the Thames into which it drained, were ideal for the growth of old Roman London. The river's wellspring was in what is now Shoreditch churchyard, marked by a pump.

A little more specifically, the remains of wooden trackways which were discovered just beyond the River Lea have been dated to 4000 BC (i.e. before the end of the Stone Age). These would certainly have been to enable travellers to cross the marshes and would have given hunters easier access to the rich wildlife. Incidentally, the *East London Advertiser* featured a Neolithic site uncovered in 2016 during a geophysics survey around Victoria Park between Old Ford and Hackney during Crossrail investigations. This details the existence of ninety stone monoliths between 20ft and 30ft high dating back 2,500 years before Stonehenge, in a circle four times its size. Sadly, the report is dated 1 April.

During the late Stone Age, and the Bronze Age which followed, any burgeoning society would not have been secular as it is today – we are talking of a primitive people more likely to be interested in looking after their gods and their dead than themselves, evidenced by burials accompanied by the practicalities of pots and flints for the journey.

The dead and the great rivers were powerful spiritual forces between 4000 and 1500 BC, a time when plants were being cultivated, animals tamed, stones shaped, and when fire was being used to turn local clay into pots and rock into molten metal. Gifts of food, pots and flint and metal tools were placed in the river to honour spirits and ancestors, the reason why the Thames has been such a lucrative source of prehistoric finds, preserved by the wet conditions which excluded oxygen and prevented decay.

A number of archaeological surveys (see the Bibliography) explain how the lower sea level of the River Lea in the Bronze Age would have allowed exploitation and occupation of the riverbanks and the small islands within its boundaries as well as providing a navigable route.

FINDERS (NOT KEEPERS)

Locally, early finds – from the late Bronze Age and early Iron Age – were generally predictable: fragments of a jar found during excavations on Stepney High Street in the 1970s, for instance, and 'worked' flints revealed in a 1989 Limehouse dig. The Blackwall burial mentioned from the Stone Age had struck flints and pottery nearby, as well as yet more pottery fragments from the Bronze Age, along with early evidence of cereal growing. One stone axe-head from Blackwall on display in the Museum of London is dated between 4000 and 2200 BC. Interestingly, Samuel Pepys wrote in his diary (22 September 1665) of the remains of an ancient forest here.

Not far away, in the Liverpool Street area, the twenty-first-century Crossrail development has unearthed plenty of Bronze Age tools, as well as Stone Age artefacts from other parts of the City and East London including the jaw bone of a mammoth found under Canary Wharf (on the Isle of Dogs) which dates from 100,000 to 200,000 years ago. A piece of amber found at this particular site is estimated by archaeologists to be 55 million (yes, million) years old!

Stone Age and Bronze Age trackways, along with wood peats, have been revealed at excavations (by the Museum of London Archaeology Service) on Atlas Wharf on the Isle of Dogs, the trackways crossing a major channel of the Thames where fast-flowing water predominated. The Thames Valley Archaeological Service has published details (in 2000) of prehistoric finds close by at Westferry Road, including the fragmented remains of the rear left leg of a horse, with other species such as cattle, sheep, goats and even a pig represented, seemingly domesticated species from a human settlement. This site also unearthed fragments of a copper alloy brooch and earrings which could date back as far as the Iron Age. Interestingly, the later, badly eroded, Roman pottery found here was in worse condition than the prehistoric. More generally, archaeologists believe that a large network of timber pathways was constructed across East London in the Bronze Age, allowing easier access for hunters to the abundant wildlife that would have lived on what was lush wetlands thousands of years ago.

Finds of animal bones in the Victoria Park area show that ancient Britons in this location were meat-eaters, and vegetation evidence shows a farming society as early as 3000 BC. Until further archaeological digs are authorised, nothing more specific is accessible.

It is believed that this wild landscape East of London (before there was a London) was tamed to some extent from around 1500 BC. It seems that the local gravelly soil, lightly wooded with open spaces, was not just fertile but easily cleared to produce timber for building and to grow corn. A plentiful supply of water from local springs and wells in addition to the rivers has been identified, adding to its potential. There is an impressive long bronze sword dating from 1150 BC in the Museum of London that was found at Millwall in 1835. Its grip, which would have been of wood or bone, had disintegrated as a result of its handling at that time, but what remains is attributed to a 'warrior elite'.

It is the Tower Hill area, bordering what is now the East End, where a Bronze Age burial of cremated human remains was found together with a later Iron Age burial. Hundreds of years later, the first proper settlements in what became London are all believed to be on high ground above the water line, atop hills such as Tower Hill. Roman scribes wrote of warlike tribes defending their timber fortresses with ditches. Certainly, there were tribes settling all over Britain in the years before the Romans came, with communities in places like St Alban's, Colchester and Canterbury, influenced by the Druids and their organised priesthood and by the later Celts. There are accounts of a Belgic tribe moving along the Thames and then the River Lea from their native Belgium in 50 BC (the Lea being effectively the eastern boundary of the real East End in contemporary thinking) ,although they seem to have settled a little further north.

MAYBE IT'S BECAUSE I'M A LONDONER ...

The Tower Hamlets area would have been part of the territory of the Catuvellauni, a powerful Celtic tribe who invaded in the second century BC and who put up a strong resistance first to Julius Caesar on his expeditions in 55 and 54 BC and, of course, to the Romans who followed in his footsteps.

Roman map. *Tower Hamlets Record Office*

It was the arrival of the Romans in AD 43 that facilitated the growth of London, growing up around the banks of the Thames which rose in the swampy area now better known as Shoreditch. The founding of London (or Londinium, to use an earlier name) is regarded by many as being a stop-off route for the Romans between landing points in Kent and the garrison town of Colchester in Essex, a military encampment in a sparsely populated valley. In 1972 a defensive ditch (complete with a buried Roman sword) was located in the Aldgate area, probably constructed before any Roman roads. Although the location of the first crossing across the Thames has never been authenticated, it seems that the riverbank would have been less marshy in Roman times at the point around where the Tower of London now stands, not far from Aldgate. Certainly, a suitable and substantial crossing would have been a military necessity.

The original development (hardly a town at that stage) was pretty much wiped out by Boudicca and her tribe less than twenty years later, necessitating its rebuilding. This same area – more specifically Trinity Place, near Tower Hill tube station – was the location of a funerary monument dedicated to Classicianus, the man employed to revive Londinium after Boudica's attempt at devastation – he died in AD 65 and the remains of his tomb can be seen at the British Museum.

Boudicca would almost certainly have had to cross the River Lea on her way to London. She and her 100,000 supporters – men, women and children – must have been an amazing sight for the few 'locals'! She and the Romans are presumed to have used the Old Ford (the name still used) to cross the river, with a Roman road built in the area within ten years of their arrival and which lives on as … 'Roman Road'. The original road is likely to have reached Londinium at one end and the site of Boudicca's Iceni tribe (near Norwich) at the other.

It was no doubt the Romans who brought stone by barge from quarries in Kent for a defensive wall around Londinium, once the settlement grew into being the Roman capital by the early part of the third century AD. The newly built (or rebuilt) wall has been calculated as being 9ft thick, 22ft high and 3 miles long, guarded by fifteen towers each 40ft high, with five gates giving access to the major military roads. Londinium remained the Roman capital until their empire crumbled *c*. AD 410, when the town was almost literally abandoned.

Shoreditch High Street is one thoroughfare that started life as a Roman road, leading from Bishopsgate through East London up to Lincoln, often following the course of the River Lea – the name Ermine Street is used for the road, although this name is not Roman, but derived from a later

Saxon name. Another Roman road led to Ratcliff, mooted as a suitable place for landing ships, with easy access to the Thames. This road evolved into Ratcliff Highway and subsequently The Highway.

More specifically, archaeologists during excavations in 2002–3 identified 'a major Roman road' running from east to west between The Highway and Cable Street, with an extensive Roman settlement 'the size of a small town' either side of Wapping Lane to the south of this road. A large bath house was discovered here, and the settlement was the source of some fascinating artefacts, not just pottery but golden jewellery and even a stove. An impressive dwelling suggests a major status building, perhaps a palace or military headquarters, with a Roman version of under-floor heating. Scattered oyster shells and geese, ox and beef carcasses give some idea of diet. The building was constructed of stone, i.e. was not intended as a temporary structure, and boasted the remains of what seems to have been a plunge pool. Timber buildings, clay and plaster walls and floors, the remains of wall paintings, coins and hairpins were also recovered nearby. The Romans' perceived interest in spas and bathing was also endorsed by scraps of leather garments found nearby and described as being 'bikini' style with side ties. The author of *Underground London* speculates that this particular garment might have belonged to a female acrobat or even a gladiatrix at a Roman gladiator games, although no amphitheatre remains have been found (yet!) in this part of London.

BROWN BREAD (DEAD!) ROMANS

Burials were not permitted within the city walls by the Romans, hence the large graveyard discovered just outside the walls near Liverpool Street Station and stretching from Bishopsgate as far as Spitalfields. It was in the Spitalfields cemetery in 1999 that the late Roman sarcophagus, lead coffin, skeleton and artefacts of a young woman were unearthed. The Museum of London experts are convinced that this was a high-ranking female, given the evidence of gold thread and silk fragments and the presence of jet and glass trinkets. The scallop-shell design on the coffin lid indicated pagan belief in the underworld. Subsequent DNA tests have traced the woman to the Basque area of Spain. The skeleton of a child was also found in a nearby burial chamber, with an unparalleled array of glass vessels, also suggesting perhaps high status and indicating that this part of the cemetery could have been reserved for the higher echelons of Roman society. Some 150 Roman graves were found on the Spitalfields site, a quarter of them accompanied by grave goods such as jars, phials, beakers, wooden boxes or shale bracelets, one even with a chicken – for lunch on the onward journey?

Prescot Street, Aldgate, has revealed a significant number of Roman burials (more than 550) over the years, most of them accompanied by drinking vessels, with all that implies. A 2009 dig here uncovered a rare multi-coloured glass dish regarded as very expensive (worth many times the annual salary of a Roman soldier), part of grave goods in a wooden container. Human remains dating back to the first century AD have also been found close by in North Tenter Street, Alie Street and Mansell Street, suggesting a number of perhaps smaller cemeteries, with a range of artefacts surfacing, from a figurine of Venus to a late Roman official-looking belt. The diverse remains of hobnail shoes, a shale bracelet, glass beads and half of an inscribed gravestone were found in Hooper Street in 1988, just yards to the east, plus, of particular interest, a jet pendant in a grave, something often used to accompany burials because it was thought to have magic properties, and to protect the dead on their final journey. A flint structure found in East Tenter Street unearthed the same year may well have been part of a mausoleum. Exceptional finds (in Prescot Street), according to the London Archaeological Archive, were three unusual flagons which seem to have served a ritual or religious function. This whole area was known as Goodman's Fields. A particularly detailed green marble tablet was dug up here in 1787, inscribed to the memory of Flavius Agricola of the Sixth Legion – 'an incomparable husband'. (The Sixth Legion arrived in Britain in

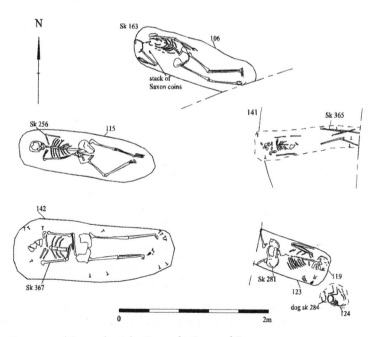

Roman and Saxon burials. *From the Steward Street report*

AD 119, led by the Emperor Hadrian.) As for the coffins themselves, these were mostly wooden so only traces survive, with the exception of some lead reinforcing strips found at West Tenter Street, displayed in the Museum of London.

Cremations have been unearthed a little further east at a Shadwell cemetery, dating back to the second century AD, and Roman coffins were discovered in Stepney in the seventeenth century and in Bethnal Green in the nineteenth, with evidence suggesting that there were more cremations than inhumations in Roman times. There was an article in the *Illustrated London News* of 5 April 1862 as follows:

As Mr Buckmaster, weaver, living at No. 13 Camden Gardens, Bethnal Green Road, was digging in a corner of his garden on the 8th ult., he uncovered a leaden coffin about 4ft from the surface. In endeavouring to lift the lid, he broke off almost a third part of it. The coffin was nearly filled with lime, through which a portion of a human skeleton appeared. Mr Rolfe of Bethnal Green, who describes the coffin, says that the contents had been greatly disturbed before he saw it, but from the lid alone he declared it to be Roman. The sides are plain, the ends have a well-known ornament, an X, and on each side an I ... Instead of the usual cord or bead and two-line pattern, generally seen on Roman coffins, the double lines in this example are joined by curves turned inward, having the appearance of the spinal column of some fish, or a close-jointed bamboo. The left upper limb of the cross alone has three lines between the curves. There is no further ornament beyond a border of the same pattern around the overlapping lid. The dimensions are length 5ft 10in, breadth at the head 1ft 4in, at the foot 1ft 2in, depth about 10in. The weight is estimated at 4 cwt. There was an outer coffin of oak.

There were two jet hairpins in this coffin.

At the Tower Hamlets Local History Archive is a paper from the *Proceedings of the Society of Antiquarians* in June 1910, detailing the discovery of a number of Roman burials in the area. Of these, the most detailed information is provided with regard to a coffin discovered in 1856 at 'Mr Hemmings Iron Church and House Works' in Bow, just north of Bow Road, having been broken in pieces by workmen. This was identified as Roman partly because of the use of lime to cover the skeleton, a fairly common practice at the time, though there has been some debate as to whether this was to preserve the remains or hasten their decomposition!

WHAT THE ROMANS LEFT BEHIND

There have been archaeological excavations in many parts of the East End, revealing far more than endless burials. One of these was the remains of a Roman civilian settlement found at Old Ford flanking both sides of the Roman road which led from London to Colchester, crossing the River Lea. Here were discovered the bones of cattle, which, together with the land's historic fertility, evidence a farming community. (Some historians feel that the large amount of cattle butchering that was revealed indicated a level of surplus that could be sold in the larger settlements in what became London.)

In Armagh Road, Bow, a 1990 dig uncovered a quarry believed to have supplied rock for the Romans, but with additional evidence of plough-soil from farming during that period. Some twenty years earlier in Bow, Roman pottery remains had already been discovered.

It is also interesting to speculate about objects found in Mansell Street, Aldgate, especially with regard to the identity of the owners of the silver brooch, bone comb and the bronze belt and crossbow brooch, dating back to Roman times, but, according to the Museum of London, with a style appropriate for a high-ranking German. A German serving in the Roman army or Roman government – and his wife?

Although Roman tiles have been unearthed in various locations over the years, e.g. in the reconstruction of St Dunstan's Church in Stepney in 1885, it has been established that such tiles were often re-used and do not indicate a Roman settlement. The area around St Dunstan's, however, between two Roman roads, on high fertile ground only a mile inland from the 'port' at Ratcliff, seems more likely than most for Roman development.

At Shadwell, the remains of what may have been a Roman signal station have been found, a good location for a look-out for enemy ships approaching London, although the area would have been affected by the dramatic drop in water levels during the Roman occupation, i.e. from first to fifth centuries AD. Some theories in recent years actually suggest that this structure was more likely to be a mausoleum, and as more and more archaeological discoveries are made no doubt further evidence and fresh theories will surface.

Nearby on the Isle of Dogs, the wall of 'Millwall' was a great bank of stones and earth dating back to the Romans. A natural phenomena, it kept the River Thames from flooding at high tide, allowing the land to be cultivated as farmland. Roman deposits the other side of what is now Millwall Inner Dock (i.e. the Isle of Dogs) have also suggested the presence of an inhabited farm, although persistent flooding could have made this short-lived. The routes of the Roman roads out of Londinium and into Essex were ideal for corn-fields and market gardens, with fertile soil, and space for meadows for the animals.

Aldgate, however, started life as just that: a gate – one of the original Roman gates erected (*c.* AD 190) around the city, this one dividing Londinium from the East End and guarding the road to Colchester. The others were around what is now the City of London, and all provided

Saxon carving in St Dunstan's. *Hornbeam Arts, via Flickr*

rooftop platforms which could be used for catapulting machines, an effective defence. Any archaeological remnants of the Roman gate have long been obscured, and there is now no evidence of its original exact location, but it is believed to have straddled what is now Aldgate High Street. In the 1603 *A Survay [sic] of London,* John Stow refers to the gate as originally having had two portcullises, lowered at night to protect the city.

North of here at Spitalfields was the area said to have supplied the soil (brick-earth) for the Romans to build floors and walls and to make bricks and tiles. Gravel was also quarried in Spitalfields to make the famous Roman roads, and timber-lined wells have been found here containing Roman pots which seem to have been dumped there when the well was no longer in use, presumably as some kind of religious offering.

AND NOT FAR AWAY

The Crossrail development and its historic finds at Liverpool Street are just over the borders defined by this book, but there is one particular find which is so unusual, and which says so much about Roman life, that it is impossible to exclude it. This was the discovery of an iron shackle which archaeologists are convinced was related to the keeping of prisoners or slaves in Roman London. Some such slaves were brought from Rome with their 'masters' but others would have been captured Britons, with some of course going on to be gladiators. The nearest Roman amphitheatre to the East End which has been unearthed is below the Guildhall in the City of London, which also makes it the nearest potential site for gladiatorial games, with the broken bones and decapitated skulls of young men discovered nearby as 'evidence'.

It was during the fourth century AD that the Roman Empire was in trouble thanks to civil wars at 'home' and German and

Aldgate. *From Thomas Allen, The History and Antiquities of London, Westminster, Southwark and Parts Adjacent (London, 1827)*

Danish warriors raiding the British Isles, arriving by sea in their wooden boats. Their defensive walls became vulnerable, food became scarce, their economy collapsed, and Roman generals took the decision to pull out their legions, leaving many of their buildings to fall into decay in and around Londinium. A new era of pagan Saxon rule began.

2

SAXONS AND VIKINGS

After the Romans effectively abandoned London, returning to Italy following attacks there by the Visigoths (nomadic German people who had fought against Roman rule, helping to bring about the downfall of the Roman Empire), they left the original Celts to their own devices, including those east of the London settlement of course. Seeing that Britain was now undefended, the Saxons from Germany and the Angles and Jutes from Denmark arrived, first as raiders, then as settlers, and Londinium became Lundenwic, or Lundwic, the first major 'Anglo-Saxon' settlement; becoming a centre for international trade by the eighth century, including the slave trade. However, it seems that most of the new arrivals did not seem to be interested in urban life and were apparently wary of the ruins left behind in Londinium, establishing themselves in the main outside the city walls in more rural areas, even if such areas were wooded or marshy, like Stepney. Whether there were concerns about the area being haunted (given the Saxons' pagan beliefs) or more practical concerns about maintaining the infrastructure is not known.

From the middle of the seventh century, however, the original Roman London was gradually redeveloped around the Covent Garden/Strand area – the 'wic' of Lundenwic meaning market. Unfortunately, the only Saxon structure found within the original Roman walls is the Saxon doorway and a fragment of pavement in All Hallows by the Tower, the oldest church in London, pre-dating the Tower itself by 400 years, and just west of the area now known as the East End (the church, incidentally, was first established in 675 by the Anglo-Saxon abbey at Barking in Essex, and originally named All Hallows, Barking). There have also been intermittent discoveries of Saxon pottery, coins, jewellery and combs within the walls, on the banks of the Thames, including late Saxon brooches from Germany and Sweden, further evidence of trade. Similarly, there have been finds of the essentials used by weavers, dating back to the 700s, suggesting cloth production there at that time, no doubt not just for local use.

East of the walls is largely unexplored and the Saxons left little behind for historians to investigate. For example, there are a number of historic references to Whitechapel Mount being part of some kind of Saxon defence system – it was depicted as being a large hillock, with footpaths to the top, where the Royal London Hospital is now – but no real evidence that this was the case, or how old it is.

WHAT'S IN A NAME?

The plethora of Saxon names in what is now the East End do appear to substantiate the settlement of many of these newcomers in the area. The River Lea (or Lee) itself is from the Saxon *lygan* (fast flowing). Cambridge Heath is possibly from a Saxon called Centbeorht, Wapping from a Saxon called Waeppa or from *wapol*, meaning marsh, Bethnal Green from *blithehale* (happy corner!) or 'Blida's' corner, Bromley-by-Bow from *brembel*, a field of brambles, and Shoreditch from *soersditch* (sewer ditch) with Hoxton (just north of Bethnal Green) in the Domesday Book as an Anglo-Saxon farm belonging to Hocq. While Shadwell is supposedly named after a mineral spring dedicated to the seventh-century East Saxon bishop St Chad, this has been questioned by some historians, with some of the view that the name originates partly from the old English word *ceald* for cold! As for Aldgate, the area around the original gate in the Roman wall, although 'ald' has been construed as 'old' it could also be argued to mean 'foreign', i.e. the place where foreigners passed through to get to London.

As for the origins of the name Stepney, there are a number of Saxon options – the landing place of Stebba or Styba (hence Stybbanhythe) or Stephen, or the home of Stebba's people, or a timber wharf from the word *steb* for tree – enough to perhaps suggest that Stepney could have been the first, and most substantial, Saxon settlement.

There is an interesting legend attached to the origins of what is now White Horse Lane in Stepney. The story goes that a Kentish warrior chief was killed fighting the Danes on the river during one of the Viking invasions and his body was taken to hallowed ground alongside the first incarnation of St Dunstan's Church (perhaps a simple chapel). In commemoration, the well-known badge of Kent, the white horse, was erected in some form nearby. Statue? Carving? Painting? Imagination is needed for this one but legends are more often based on truth than not.

LET'S NOT TALK ABOUT THOSE BURNT CAKES

After plague and a series of fires in Lundenwic, Alfred the Great – who had extended the port facilities – recaptured the town in 886 from the persistently invading Vikings in the Battle of London, defeating a Danish garrison. Lundenwic now became Lundenburg (meaning the fortified town of London). Alfred played a significant role in continuing with the rebuilding of London west of the city walls, and became the first of the various Anglo-Saxon rulers to be accepted as king, rather than merely king of Wessex, one of seven Anglo-Saxon kingdoms. He was also one of the only kings to have been called 'the Great'. However, when a particularly aggressive flotilla of Danes arrived by river some seven years later, London was repeatedly attacked, with a war zone effectively established between London and the River Lea, the dividing line between the Saxons to the west and the Danes to the east. The Danish territory east of the Lea was known as the Danelaw and villages nearby were avoided by travellers, and to some extent presumably by settlers. Alfred took his army from London through what is now the East End to Benfleet in Essex, further east along the Thames, to destroy the Danish camp and repel the invaders. His defeat of the Danes at Benfleet in 893 created a period of relative stability for a century, and some historians refer to Danes settling down and inter-marrying with the Saxons.

This time of peace would have been helped by Alfred's establishment of warships guarding the coast and the fortresses near the River Lea a few miles north. The *East London Observer* of 11 August 1894 has an article which also points out that Alfred 'ordered channels to be cut by which the current of the Lea was diverted and the depth reduced'. The unknown writer quotes from John Stow's 1615 *Annals: or General Chronicle of England*, which explains that this move was 'soe that where shippes before had sayled, now a small boate could scantily rowe'. This would have left Danish ships 'so much aground' that their return to the Lea mouth and into the Thames was 'rendered impracticable'. The BBC's website refers to Alfred as having established 'a navy for use against the Danish raiders' and Harold Hills goes further, in the *East London Advertiser* of 27 April 1901, suggesting that it was Alfred who actually launched some of his ships from the river banks of East London.

It is also Alfred who has been credited with the origins of the name Tower Hamlets (and other parts of East London including West Ham, Dagenham) although the Tower (of London) was not constructed until 200 years later so this may well be erroneous.

King Alfred statue, Wantage. *'Ballista', from the English Language Wikipedia (GNU Free Documentation Licence)*

It is true, however, that the word *ham* is Saxon for house, and it was Alfred who divided 'his' land into counties and shires, subdivided into 'hundreds'. East London was in the hundred of Ossulstone (a corruption of Oswald's Stone, a pre-Roman monolith which once stood where Marble Arch is now), and each hundred consisted of 100 hams, each ham with 100 Saxon thanes who paid 'suit and service' (i.e. homage) at the Hundred Court. These details are supplied by historian Charles McNaught, writing in the *East London Observer* on 23 April 1910, and of course East Ham, West Ham etc. are still in existence. Thanes in Anglo-Saxon times were the forerunner of the upper classes, and played a part in the evolution of the English justice system. They were required to furnish men and means for the king's government and defence, with their hams evolving into homesteads and thence to villages.

SETTLING DOWN WITH A NICE CUP OF TEA

There seems to be evidence of a Viking encampment at nearby Hackney at this time (the remains of a Saxon boat being found here), with an Anglo-Saxon settlement a few miles east at Bow, such settlements being primitive and in contrast to the Roman structures. Any housing would have been made of wood, explaining the difficulties for archaeologists. Poplar, Limehouse and Wapping, in addition to Stepney, were likely to have had small Saxon communities, with the Saxons thought to have built dykes alongside the Thames to cope with flooding at high tide – the Romans having mainly avoided such low-lying areas. Blackwall is said to have derived its name from one such dyke, or wall, of black mud, with Millwall and Wapping other likely sites. As for Stepney itself, there are stories of a Saxon warrior called Stibba landing in the Limehouse area where Dunbar Wharf is now and rowing inland up a navigable channel known as the Black Ditch. That channel continued through what is now Bethnal Green and terminated in the Shoreditch area, perhaps where the holy well existed that lent its name to the priory built there in the twelfth century. Additionally, the Tower Hamlets council website refers to a thriving suburb in Saxon times around the 'stone' Whitechapel, and there are scattered references elsewhere to this location revealing a 'Saxon pit' and barricade, and a 'penny of Alfred'.

Author Jane Cox surmises that Stepney Church (now St Dunstan's) began life under the Saxons as an outpost of St Paul's, with farmers and millers paying rent to their bishops. Certainly, the manor of Stepney was given to the Bishop of London as his diocese in 604 and this area would have stretched from Aldgate to the River Lea and from Muswell Hill in north London to the River Thames, a substantial territory with an unknown number of parishes. In *Old East Enders*, Cox gives an evocative description of thatched huts, cattle enclosures and a dense woodland hunting ground to the north (the area now part of Victoria Park) with swine rooting for acorns – and why not? Similarly, in *From Ice Age to Essex* the Museum of London Archaeology Service describes early Saxon settlements in East London as 'undefended villages and farmsteads concentrated along the Thames and its tributaries'.

THE ARGY BARGY

During the reign of Alfred's descendant Edgar (959–975) he was petitioned by thirteen knights to grant them the wasteland to the east of the city wall. In John Stow's *Survay* [*sic*] *of London* (1598) this request is described as conditional, requiring the knights to accomplish 'three combats' on a particular day in East Smithfield – one above ground, one below, and one in the water, then running 'with spears against all comers', which they duly accomplished. As a result the knights involved were granted that portion of land known then as all East Smithfield to include the 'new ditch of the Tower' and down to St Katharine's Hospital (the precursor of St Katharine Docks). The portion of land – a rough area, the alleged haunt of robbers – was renamed the Knighten Guild, and latterly Portsoken Ward. The recently named Knighten Street in Wapping is a nod to this guild of knights who may have taken on the role of policing the area in some way.

In 994, the Viking attacks returned and continued, with the English King Ethelred trying to stop them by offering gold and land (Danegeld), a tactic which failed miserably. Things came to a head when Canute (or Cnut) and his Danish army of 10,000 men in 200 longships arrived in 1015. He defeated King Edmund (Ethelred's son), who ceded him all the territory north of the Thames, which included what is now Tower Hamlets, with Canute 'inheriting' the crown and the rest of England when Edmund died soon after. The new king, although a renowned and seemingly fierce Viking warrior, actually seems to have united the Danes and the English using cultural bonds rather than brutality, and had a long reign by the standards of the day (over nineteen years) as the one-and-only English king. He certainly seems to have encouraged trade with Scandinavia, although this seems to have included the slave trade, with reports that his sister-in-law bought pretty English slave girls to sell in Denmark (most servants and farm workers around this time were slaves). However, during his reign, the city now known as London grew in importance to such an extent that it took over from Winchester as the capital of England.

A BIT OF RELIGION

Although no doubt starting life as a wooden structure, it seems that by AD 1000 Stepney Church had been rebuilt in stone. Being close to the port of Ratcliff, many sailors were buried there, leading to it later becoming known as the Church of the High Seas. An eleventh-century crude stone crucifix in what became the more solid east wall can still be seen, establishing its antiquity, and its presence would have been important at a time when Christianity was slowly replacing paganism with its plethora of gods.

Vikings. *Public domain painting by Oscar Wergeland on Wikimedia Commons*

The tenth-century St Dunstan started life in humble circumstances but became Bishop of London, a powerful politician, lord of Stepney Manor and, latterly, the patron saint of the Goldsmiths' Company in London. Some historians feel that he lived in what was then Stepney at Bishop's Hall (a later name), now where the Museum of Childhood (in Bethnal Green) is located. By the time he died in 988, he was Archbishop of Canterbury, and it is said that he worked to bring the Saxons, Angles and Danes together to live in peace. He also tried to reform church morals by insisting on the poverty, chastity and obedience of monks and celibacy of the parish priests. Dunstan himself was a cultured man with a perhaps unexpected interest in metalwork, the latter hobby having spawned a legend regarding him tweaking the devil's nose with red-hot tongs – certainly a patron saint with a difference.

As for the church, it seems to have started life as a chapel for the welfare of local dwellers near the river. It was built on the track that led from the Bishop's Hall, crossing what is now Old Ford Road, to the river – it was commonplace that the oldest roads led to the river. This original track would probably have followed what is now Globe Road, Whitehorse Lane and Whitehorse Street to the Ratcliff port, but the chapel would have been beyond the marshland to make it suitable for Christian burials. It was dedicated originally to All Saints but subsequently to St Dunstan after his canonisation.

There is some further information regarding Stepney Church in nineteenth-century copies of *St Dunstan's Magazine*. In 1882, for instance, a Mr A.M. Barnard writes of a spire atop the church tower built 'in 958 by Dunstan, who raised up a new church on the site of another, which was one of the oldest Christian buildings in the country'. In 1883, another anonymous writer refers to the revival of Christianity in Saxon times, 'the result of the Italian mission headed by Augustine ... even a thousand years ago there must have been some kind of representative of the ancient but comparatively modern building in which we now worship'. Augustine was the late sixth-century missionary sent by the pope to convert the Anglo-Saxons to Christianity: the man who became the first Archbishop of Canterbury. Additionally, the following anonymous articles appeared in the *East London Advertiser* as detailed:

30 April 1903
Stepney, in Saxon and Norman times, was a place of some note; coins are occasionally met with which were struck in the mint at Stepney, both by Saxon and Norman kings. And in many ways Stepney was a place of importance and

therefore a place which Dunstan would be likely to patronise. [*Note: there is no confirmed evidence of a mint at Stepney, and this has possibly been confused with the mint at Stafford – one of seventy Saxon mints – thanks to the ancient script on the coins. However, there do seem to have been several unidentified places minting coins 'in London' by the ninth century, so Stepney was a possibility.*]

9 April 1910:

St. Dunstan's, Stepney, is one of the most interesting churches in Greater London. It is the Mother Church of East London, and was in Saxon times the only church between the Walls of London and the River Lea on the East, and between the Thames and Hackney on the North. The Tower of London itself is in Stepney Deanery, and the Tower Hamlets were the early centres of village life out of which has grown the vast city we now call the East End. In this large area, at first of course sparsely populated, St. Dunstan's was the only church. The date of its first building is unknown, and its first dedication, to All Saints, is largely a matter of tradition. Dunstan, Bishop of London in 959, is said to have rebuilt the church and after his death in 988 and canonisation, his name was added to the dedication. So the full name of the church now is All Saints' and St. Dunstan's but it is interesting to know that the dedication festival is still kept on All Saints Day, November 1st.

The origins of St Botolph-without-Aldgate could date back even further, perhaps to the tenth century, because burials from this date have been found in its crypt. St Botolph was a seventh-century saint (died *c.* 680), the patron saint of travellers, and St Botolph Church would have been the ideal resting place for travellers in and out of early London.

The reference to 'without-Aldgate' indicates the church's location outside the Roman walls. Similarly, St Leonard's in Shoreditch has a history dating back to the twelfth century, but is believed to have had an earlier Anglo-Saxon incarnation. The site of what became Holy Trinity Priory just west of Aldgate in Norman times has been identified as that of an eleventh-century cemetery, probably associated with a long-lost (unknown) church. Sadly, the possible Saxon roots – including Saxon artefacts – of the original chancel of the Church of St Leonard's Convent in Bromley-by-Bow were destroyed when the church was bombed during the Second World War.

SAILORS, FARMERS AND WHEELER DEALERS

The settlement at Stepney would have grown gradually in all directions around St Dunstan's. The area down to the riverside was then (i.e. by the year 1000) a separate hamlet called Ratcliff, where a small port developed, with local cottages inhabited by fishermen and ferrymen. Ratcliff had a gravel shoreline suitable for landing, one of the few below the Roman-built London Bridge. The 'waterfront' was gradually improved by building wooden embankments east and west of London's walls; it is quite likely that small-scale Saxon open boats sold goods at the riverside and their craft were unsophisticated and designed to be pulled up onto a 'beach'. Certainly the locals seemed more interested in maintaining their boats than their roads, which struggled to retain Roman standards, but this is no doubt partly due to the fact that boats were the only form of transport: possession of a horse and cart was very rare indeed. Water transport would have been used for freshwater and marine fishing, for communication with different regions and for trade – including overseas trade.

In March 1863, Rev. Canon Stanley gave a talk about London's history to the St Philip's (Stepney) Working Men's Institute and touched on the subject of the Saxons, mentioning that the Poplar area was named after the trees that proliferated there at that time. He also mentions Stepney Church as being originally called All Saints, which he believed to be a Saxon name (his talk was reported in the *East London Observer* of 28 March 1863). Eleven years later, a Professor Brewer spoke about 'Ancient London' to the Working Men's Institute, pointing out that the Anglo-Saxons seemed to prefer life as shepherds, swineherds and beekeepers 'in the green fields' and 'beneath the shade of the broad oaks in the forest' to 'standing behind a counter, and selling cloth in the booths in the town'. So the fields, woods and open spaces making up East London would have been ideal (as reported in the *East London Observer*, 11 April 1874).

Other generic sources also foreground the Saxons as having uncomplicated lifestyles, only in need of food, shelter and warmth, and there is certainly a general consensus that neither incoming Anglo-Saxons nor locals were in any way literate. Nevertheless, the writings of the Venerable Bede (*c.* 673–735), and particularly his *The Ecclesiastical History of the English People*, are often the reference point for much Anglo-Saxon history; he wrote of London at that time being the 'metropolis of the East Saxons' with 'many nations' trading by sea and land. Certainly the River Thames would have been instrumental for trading, and London's fortifications made life difficult for invaders, with the seafaring settlers building ships here and elsewhere. The East End's borders with not just one but two rivers made it instrumental in Saxon trading.

SOME DEAD BODIES

In the Tower Hamlets Archive there is a particularly detailed report from the London & Middlesex Archaeological Society, dated 2009, by Simon Cass and Steve Preston, which details both Roman and Saxon burials in Steward Street, Spitalfields. This followed excavations by the Thames Valley Archaeological Services in 2006. One of the Saxon burials was carbon-dated to between 774 and 1017, and was buried with eighth-century coins (known as sceattas). Over seventy fragments of pottery were found on site, much of it Saxon, along with Roman and Norman remains. Archaeologists seemed to have been surprised to find Saxon burials, and one particular skeleton is described in detail:

- buried face upwards;
- slightly rolled on the right side;
- face pointing south;
- left arm extended;
- right arm bent at elbow with hand resting on head;
- legs and feet parallel, knees slightly bent;
- degraded and fragile bones but approximately 90 per cent complete;
- no coffin fittings recovered;
- surfaces covered in hardened gravefill.

There is plenty of evidence of Saxon burials in the City of London, but it is limited elsewhere, so this was quite a find.

SO WHAT DID THE SAXONS LEAVE BEHIND?

Not a lot. The document referred to in the previous paragraph reports on other Saxon finds, with different digs revealing and identifying metal fragments in the nearby Thames, not far from the Tower of London – a spearhead, axe and horse stirrup. In the heart of the East End there is mention of a single bead from Brick Lane near Aldgate, and two Viking spearheads from Shadwell. Anglo-Saxon spearheads found in the Thames may have been offerings to gods to celebrate victory.

In the Museum of London a decorated mount is displayed from a dig at Smithfield, dating to the 'early 1000s' – this has a striking gilded copper alloy pattern in a typically Norwegian style called Ringerike. The display here suggests that the mount probably adorned a chest, saddle or piece of furniture. Alongside the mount is a spur, similarly dated, but found in the Canning Town area (just east of the River Lea), another decorative piece with a brass and silver inlay; bearing in mind that the first horseshoes only appeared from the 900s, it would appear that the use of horses as transport was becoming rather more sophisticated.

AND WHAT ABOUT THE WOMEN

What indeed? Saxon London was surrounded by manors under what was known as *gavelkind* – Stepney and Mile End (and nearby Hackney) included. This was common practice in Saxon times, particularly in Kent (where there were more Saxon settlements) and it meant that any estate, on death, would be divided among all the sons equally, the youngest son taking 'the homestead'. It seems that incoming Danes reserved women for various forms of service (and its various interpretations), and Anglo-Saxon laws generally did not hold women in high esteem – drowning was a popular punishment for women, the Saxons having supposedly introduced the forerunner of the ducking stool. Admittedly, the original Saxon 'cucking stool' was for men and women.

Some Saxons had arrived with multiple wives (a practice that was not uncommon), and Roman women who had been left behind were absorbed into Anglo-Saxon families. It seems that Canute actively encouraged Scandinavians to settle in London (probably inside the walls rather than outside), but the women living in the settlements that became the East End were already a diverse and multi-ethnic mixture.

3

NORMANS

JUST OVER THE BORDER

This period covers less than a century, from 1066 to 1154, kicking off with the Duke of Normandy's victory at the Battle of Hastings – of course! – and ending with the death of the last Norman king, Stephen. To be fair, Norman activity was hardly centred in and around the East End of London, although within the Roman walls was a different story. London was one place the victor – now proclaimed William I, King of England – needed to conquer after that most famous of battles. What this meant was that the isolated villages east of the walls were left less devastated by his army than the growing settlement within the walls. In fact, it seems that William's negotiating powers with the Saxon citizens had more effect than violence, and he found a variety of ways to impose his supremacy on the people, building a plethora of Norman castles and religious institutions. The closest to the East End was the White Tower, now part of the Tower of London, and just over the area's border, though not known as the White Tower until several hundred years later after it became the central keep of the Tower. The location was chosen partly because some of the city's walls at this point were collapsing, due to the changes in the tidal movement of the Thames.

The White Tower. *Author's collection*

The White Tower was under construction by the 1070s and completed by the beginning of the reign of William's son Henry I in 1100 by Norman masons and English labourers, dominating the skyline for miles around. It was not, however, the king's main residence; this was at the palace at Westminster, which he had inherited from the Anglo-Saxons. The White Tower made use of the remains of the Roman walls, standing 92ft tall, protected by ditches, with walls between 10ft and 15ft wide; originally a motte and bailey construction, its timbers were replaced by limestone between 1078 and 1097. This original tower was designed to accommodate, when necessary, William and his family and household, plus it was seen as secure enough to keep his valuables safe while providing a gateway to the capital. It became a retreat in times of civil disorder, a power base for armed men and horses, but was also intended to overawe the indigenous population and protect the city from invasion. It could also house knights if necessary. The basement (probably used initially for stores, becoming a prison by 1100 when the Bishop of Durham was incarcerated) had a winding staircase to the state apartments and to the Norman chapel of St John; religion was important to the French invaders, with knights believing they fought under the guidance of God. The White Tower remains the most complete example of a late eleventh-century fortress palace in Europe and is described by UNESCO as an outstanding example of 'innovative Norman military architecture' which expressed the permanence, power and control of the new order. The chapel of St John is the best-preserved part of the interior.

It was, of course, the settlements, or hamlets, around the Tower which gave what is now called Tower Hamlets its name.

FOR A BIT OF PEACE

Escaping to the country, in Norman times, could mean escaping to the east of the Tower. Meadows, pastures and woodland were in abundance, with fields of wheat, oats and barley, and the sight of large ploughs drawn by teams of oxen. There would have been a blip *c.* 1131 when cattle plagues wiped out many oxen, and floods affected Stepney marshland in 1099 and 1115, but such problems were par for the course for its rural residents. The Isle of Dogs was probably walled by the time of William I and used as further pasture. But the village of Stepney grew slowly, down to the riverside hamlet of Ratcliff with its developing port, scattered with cottages inhabited by fishermen and ferrymen. The gravel shoreline at Ratcliff was one of the few suitable landing places below London Bridge which was inside the London walls (London Bridge, incidentally, had started out as a primitive wooden structure until it was replaced from 1176 onwards). From Ratcliff it was an uphill walk to St Dunstan's, which was serving a population of around 500 people by 1154, drawn from surrounding hamlets.

Villagers and craftsmen would have been of old English stock, but the top religious and urban aristocratic figures were now French, as were most landholders east of London (as elsewhere). The Saxon language was kept alive among the peasants in these rural settlements but was overtaken in higher circles by Norman French, which was also used at court in addition to Latin. The struggle between the two languages continued for around 200 years. Stepney peasants would have been suspicious of new-fangled ideas about agriculture – and about religion and literacy, too. It is possible they came into contact with Norman kings hunting in the forest areas around the River Lea, but any such contact goes unrecorded.

One twelfth-century historian, Orderic Vitalis, had suggested that Norman women were too afraid of the sea crossing to join their menfolk, so men may well have outnumbered women at this time. Their lives were improving in some ways, as new Anglo-Norman rules meant they could be heiresses; but, predictably, most women would rarely stray far from home and were responsible for looking after the animals and preparing and preserving food.

THE FIRST FAMOUS BOOK

The Domesday Book was commissioned by William I because he needed taxes for his army, and so had to find out the wealth and assets of his new subjects. He sent out commissioners across the land to find out, and the results were published, in Latin, in 1086. It is of course this historic record that gives some idea of the rurality of the area, with a brief reference to the woodland and arable areas concentrated between Bethnal Green and Shoreditch. Stepney is the only part of the East End detailed in the survey, bearing in mind that even London is not included within its pages. Haggerston, part of Shoreditch, does get a mention, its land owned by Robert de Gernon, a Norman. The only East End buildings noted were Stepney's eight tidal watermills, including those at Old Ford and Wapping, of great importance to the area economically. These were isolated at the edges of a marshy landscape on the Thames, the Lea and its tribu- taries. No doubt there were

Watermill. *Motif collection*

bakehouses nearby which could have dated back this far, with Bow and Bromley-by-Bow spawning baking com- munities, not just for local consumption but for delivery to London through Aldgate. There are also some random references to mills (plural) in East Smithfield 'from King Stephen's time' e.g. in John Stow's sixteenth-century *Anglo-Saxon Chronicles*.

Mentioned in the Domesday Book are 183 peasant households; the individuals who lived in them would have been subdivided into slightly higher-status villeins (who were able to rent property), the poorer cottars, who were probably craftsmen or market gardeners, and serfs, who were freer than slaves but not treated that much better. However, the book was not a population census: the amount of 'ploughs', or land that could be ploughed, was more important than the number of people, the latter guesstimated at around 850 for the Stepney area, i.e. around five people per household. Only landowners are mentioned by name, so there is an absence of wom- en's names (although these did turn up in other parts of England) – there is a tenant listed as 'wife of Brien', however. There are more names centred around what is now Aylward Street in Stepney than elsewhere, none of them Norman. One name, with Germanic roots, was that of Hugh de Berners (Bernieres is in Normandy) who came over with the Norman invasion and held land in Essex and Cambridge, plus a mill 'on the Thames'. There is also a mention of a mill 'on the Lea' built after 1066 but before Domesday, owned by Edmund, 'son of Algot', who was potentially, like his brother Ralph, a canon of St Paul's. According to British History Online, this was a fuller's watermill, subsequently abandoned due to lack of water: fulling was a way of preparing (beating) wool for cloth-making, dating back to Roman times. The Domesday Book records water-powered mills in the Bromley-by-Bow area.

A more important consideration at the time was a reference to pannage (pig pasture) for 500 pigs within the area's 7,000 acres – although the 'manor of Stepney' would then have included Hackney, Clerkenwell and Islington. Peasant houses were shared with animals and were of course made of wood, wattle and mud, needing frequent rebuilding – though not as often as those in London in the eleventh and twelfth centuries, often damaged by fire and gales. With pasture and pannage more than enough for local needs, there would have been hay and timber to spare. Interestingly, the words 'cow' and 'sheep' seem to have been Saxon names given by the poor who tended the animals, while the terms 'beef' and 'mutton' are of Norman origin, given by the Norman barons who ate them. The Norman bishop – another William – held the manor of Stepney and he and his tenants had seven mills; plus he is believed to have had a manor house in the area.

A later version of a fulling mill from a 1661 *Engraving in Theatrum Machinarum Novum, public domain Wikimedia Commons*

GET THEE TO A ...

In what was then Stratford-at-Bow, St Leonard's nunnery was founded between 1086 and 1122 by the Bishop of London for a prioress and nine Benedictine nuns, its farmland and watermills providing an income for its occupants. A monastic life would have been preferable to domesticity for some women because it offered security. The small priory chapel became the parish church, allegedly retaining some Norman architecture, mainly attributed to the arch at the west end. The site is now occupied by the derelict churchyard of the parish church of Bromley St Leonard, known as St Mary's (destroyed during the Second World War), between the busy Blackwall Tunnel Approach Road and Bromley High Street. Similarly, by the beginning of the twelfth century, the Isle of Dogs had a chapel of its own, leading to an assumption that there must have been a small settlement in this area.

On Aldgate's doorstep, Holy Trinity Priory was the first religious house to be established within London's walls after the Norman conquest, founded by Queen Matilda, wife of Henry I, *c.* 1107. It was a more prosperous venture than the convent at St Leonard's, partly from being gifted a decade or two later with the strip of land alongside (later known as Portsoken), which was no longer needed by the city's knights for defensive purposes. The prior then took on the responsibility for law and order in the area. The priory also acquired land in Bromley, including several mills. Interestingly, it seems that the Normans introduced the whole idea of hospitals in England.

Some of the priory's land near Aldgate became the site of a hospital for the poor, founded in 1148 by a later Queen Matilda (King Stephen's French wife), apparently as an act of remembrance for two of her children who were buried in Holy Trinity. She had already bought an adjoining vineyard and watermill, with the hospital catering for disadvantaged locals in an era before workhouses, and functioning as a small religious community. The Aldgate hospital became the Royal Hospital of St Katharine, a favourite fourth-century saint. (St Katharine's-by-the-Tower has since re-sited and lives on in the twenty-first century as a retreat in Limehouse.)

Holywell Priory popped up on the western edge of Shoreditch some time between 1127 and 1158, and eventually covered 8 acres, becoming the richest Augustinian nunnery in the country. This development would have transformed the sparsely occupied and rural area, but its earliest beginnings – the circumstances and instigator – are a matter of conjecture. Several sources claim that it was dedicated to the Virgin Mary and St John the Baptist, the site located at what is now No. 1 Shoreditch High Street. It was built near a holy well (hence Holywell Lane, etc.), which was probably a natural spring revered by pagans but with Christians preferring to believe that the saints made the water flow. Remains of this priory have been excavated in twenty-first-century Transport for London digs.

WHAT DID THE NORMANS DO FOR THE EAST END?

Perhaps not a lot, apart from the White Tower. However, it does look as if they built what became, a century later, known as King John's Palace, because, during its nineteenth-century demolition, the *Illustrated London News* (11 December 1858) gives details of its Norman origins. An anonymous writer points out the remains of Norman windows revealed at the front of the building with the moulding and traces of further windows, together with indications of Norman moulding and carved work in an oak-beamed chamber alongside the main dwelling. If the building started out as impressively as it ended up, it is interesting to speculate who might have lived there before it was built over in Tudor times.

CRIME AND PUNISHMENT

William I had introduced harsh penalties and punishments for rebels, and had to work hard to maintain law and order. The roots of local responsibility for crime prevention were rooted in Anglo-Saxon customs and continued after 1066 by the Norman rulers, who needed a system to control the largely Anglo-Saxon population. Communities, such as those in Stepney, were responsible for the behaviour of each other, and were obliged to chase after a criminal, raising a 'hue and cry' if they needed help. There were few government officials and everybody knew everybody else in their immediate vicinity. Interestingly, the words justice, prison, constable, agreement, fine, court, debt and evidence were all introduced into the English legal system by the Normans. Specific records of local crimes and 'trials' up to and including the Norman period have proved impossible to trace.

The nearest real 'prison' was that in the White Tower, and its first prisoner was in 1101. This was not a local man but Ranulf Flambard, the Bishop of Durham, the chief minister for William I's son, William (Rufus) II, who was arrested and confined for embezzlement. His treatment was hardly unpleasant, however, because he was able to keep servants and have wine in his room: the wine that he used to inebriate his warders and escape! So not the most successful recommendation of the efficacy of security.

A LUCKY ACCIDENT (FOR THE LOCALS...)

Henry I's Queen Matilda (who bore the Saxon name Edith before her marriage) is also revered in tradition as a result of a fall she apparently had into the River Lea while crossing at Old Ford *c.* 1108. She was quoted as having been 'well washed', describing the crossing as 'dangerous' (*East London Observer*, 16 June 1866). It seems she was on her way to visit the nunnery at Barking, crossing a river so swollen that at least one of her attendants was said to have drowned. As the wife of Henry I, she was in a position to

Queen Matilda and King Henry. *Public domain on Wikimedia Commons (Anon., Genealogical Roll of the Kings of England, c. 1300–8)*

arrange for a stone bridge to be built close to this point. It comprised three stone arches in the shape of a bow, 'a rare piece of work for before that time its like had never been seen in England' becoming known as Bow Bridge, and giving the name, subsequently, to the area. The *East London Observer* also mentions another bridge she commissioned 'over a little brook called Chanelse-bridge [*sic*] … a mile distant'. (Channelsea was a tributary of the Lea.) The anonymous writer points out that she gave manors and a mill, called Wiggon Mill, to the Abbess of Barking in return for her taking on the responsibility for the repair of the bridges and a new 'gravel highway' between them – although the abbess seems to have sold these on at some point, along with the responsibility.

This route to Barking Abbey from the city would have been the same as that taken by William I, who visited after his coronation in Westminster Abbey on Christmas Day 1066. He, however, had managed to stay upright and dry.

MOVING ON

With the death of King Stephen in 1154, it is goodbye to the Normans and hello to the much longer-lasting dynasty of the Plantagenets, covering the the Middle Ages and including the ruling – and quarrelling – houses of Lancaster and York. The grandson of Henry I, the French-speaking Henry II, arrived in England, inheriting a country recovering from the fighting for supremacy that had been taking place between yet another Matilda, Henry I's daughter, and Stephen (Henry I's nephew). While this civil war had affected many in Britain, the East End came through it all unscathed. The Norman conquerors were too busy fighting off dissent in London to concern themselves with the toiling villagers in the east, and the manor of Stepney remained in the hands of the Bishop of London, who continued as the principal landowner and landlord. It is worth mentioning, too, that it seems that Stepney had acquired its first Jewish landholder, the name Salomon recorded as such in the 1140s.

Looking at the bigger picture, the Conqueror's son William Rufus had inherited the crown after his father's death in 1087, but he died in 1100, succeeded by his brother Henry I, whose only son drowned, with Henry's daughter denied the succession because many regarded a woman as 'unfit', leaving Stephen, the son of Henry's sister, as king over a divided country until his death in 1154. In the main areas of the city, west of Aldgate, London continued to grow and prosper, surviving the riots during the Matilda vs Stephen 'Anarchy', as it was later called. The creation of new wharves by Norman riverside landowners, and the increase in the size of ships arriving to unload, meant London was becoming a major port, its increased population of 10–12,000 a mixture of Normans, Saxons (the majority), French, Norwegians, Danes, Germans and Flemings. A lot had been going on! Incidentally, the Normans were said to refer to London as the Land of Sugar Cake, or *Pais de Cocaigne* in Old French, an allusion to the good life perceived there – and from that came the word Cockney.

4

THE MIDDLE AGES

A TIME OF CHANGE

Fourteen kings in little more than 300 years meant a period of turmoil and change nationally, but what about in the East End? The Church became wealthy, there were more settlers in parts of the area other than Stepney – in Poplar, on the Isle of Dogs, with overspill from the city into what became Whitechapel – and crafts were being developed in the Aldgate and East Smithfield areas: tanners, brewers, potters, brickmakers and blacksmiths among them. Peasants were finding their voice and plagues were controlling the population explosion. The further away from the city walls, the more rural the area remained, dominated by orchards, meadows and cornfields.

REVOLTING PEASANTS

In June 1381 as many as 50,000 discontented peasants from Essex and Kent besieged London and the 14-year-old King Richard II in the Tower of London, protesting against a new poll tax. The king agreed to meet them at their camp at Mile End Green to talk through their complaints, and one writer, Samantha L. Bird, refers to the dangers he, and the courtiers surrounding him, encountered en route from people pulling at his horse's bridle. His two half-brothers are said to have bolted 'across the fields of Whitechapel' to avoid the threatening mob, who were brandishing pitchforks. The king, as duly advised, fobbed the rebel army off with false promises, primarily that he would abolish the idea of serfdom and agree to peasants being able to pay their rent in cash (pence) rather than in services demanded by their landlord. One man (Wat Tyler, from Kent) was not so easily satisfied and took some of the men to Smithfield for another meeting; ending, predictably, with his death following a fracas with the Lord Mayor. Some rebels were then rounded up and hanged, but the life of the peasants began slowly to improve after this. It was the first working-class struggle for some kind of freedom and equality, and it took place in the heart of the East End, the Green described in Froissart's fourteenth-century *Chronicles* as being 'a fair place ... whereat the people of the City did sport them in the summer season'.

Less than a century later, in 1450, there was another assembly of thousands of men from Essex and Kent on Mile End Green, this time led by Jack Cade. This protest was against the corrupt court surrounding King Henry VI. The rebels attempted to take the Tower, but failed, the struggle spilling over to Mile End. At least one enemy – Henry Cromer, the Sheriff of Kent – was decapitated during the fighting at 'the field without Aldgate' (*Gregory's Chronicle*). Yet again, the rioters were defeated, this time at a battle on London Bridge, and Cade was caught and killed in Sussex, a prequel to the civil war just five years later.

Although the Wars of the Roses were not fought on the streets of London, the Tower was attacked by the Yorkists in 1461, and it was the location for a number of executions during this time of civil strife – so much so that in 1465 a scaffold and gallows were permanently erected there. Ten years later, the Lancastrian Thomas Neville brought a huge fleet into the Thames in an attempt to aid the imprisoned Lancastrian King Henry VI. His fleet moored near the Tower but, in spite of some 5,000 armed men, was unable to breach the city's defences. The rebels did, however, manage to capture the bulwark at Aldgate that the defenders had built to protect it; a battle ensued with the Londoners attacking from within and part of the garrison of the Tower coming out of a postern gate to attack the rebels in the rear. Not surprisingly, Neville's men were eventually driven back, with several hundred killed and more captured before the survivors reached their ships and escaped back to the south bank. Some did stray into the East End, though, setting fire to and looting homes and breweries at St Katharine's and at Ratcliff. Neville himself was executed a few months later, but not in the Tower; Edward IV's brother George was executed in the Tower in 1478.

MORE PEOPLE EQUALS MORE CHURCHES

The first East End churches to augment Stepney Church (St Dunstan's) were built at Bow in 1311 and in Whitechapel by 1282. There had been a chapel dedicated to St Katherine of Alexandria at one end of Bow Bridge, mentioned in 1455 as being maintained by Barking Abbey, with stories of a hermit in residence (!) but there is no further information as to when this was built. The residents of Bow had been complaining of the trudge through the winter mud to get to the mother church and had raised money to build a chapel of ease on a piece of land granted by Edward II on what was known as the King's Highway, i.e. St Mary's.

Similarly, the Whitechapel church had started life as a chapel of ease for those people who were finding the walk to St Dunstan's just too daunting. This latter church was commonly known as St Mary Matfelon (possibly named after a wealthy wine merchant and benefactor, Richard Matefelun, known to have been living locally in 1230) and was built of white chalk rubble, hence Whitechapel. It was rebuilt in 1875 and then destroyed in the Second World War, only a small park left to mark the spot. It seems likely that the Isle of Dogs also had its chapel of ease from the Middle Ages, for the same reason of convenience.

Conversely, one religious community that lost its place of worship was the Jews who had settled – in part – around Aldgate and the Tower. At the end of the thirteenth century they were expelled from the country following anti-Semitic riots (in 1215) and the destruction of a synagogue a few miles west in the City of London (1229).

THE ILLUSTRATED LONDON NEWS, JULY 24, 1875.— 93

WHITECHAPEL CHURCH OLD AND NEW.

The old Church of St. Mary Matfelon, situated in Whitechapel, at the east end of High-street, has lately been removed. It will be superseded by a new building, the main cost of which, to the extent of £12,000, is borne by the munificence of Mr. Octavius Coope, M.P. for Middlesex. Of the intended new church, as well as of the one that has disappeared, we now present an Illustration. The old church of Whitechapel was originally a chapel of ease to the parish of Stebenhith, or Stepney. The second name of this church, "Matfelon," will not be familiar or easily intelligible to most of our readers. It is, we believe, identical with a Hebrew word that signifies a woman who has become the mother of a son. There is a legend preserved by Stow, the old antiquarian writer, which has very much the cost of a fable. It is said that in 1428 there was a devout and charitable woman in this parish, who probably may not have had a son of her own, or may have had one and lost him. Indeed, she is mentioned as a widow. But she kindly adopted a young French orphan boy, and actually brought him up as her son. The French youth requited her motherly care and

OLD WHITECHAPEL CHURCH.

bounty, when he grew up to a grown manhood, by the murder of his benefactress for the purpose of getting her property. Hereupon all the in the parish assembled in right anger, seized the parricide and him with their bodkins, which was than his atrocious crime deserved. do not believe, however, that the name of St. Mary Matfelon could be de from this affair; nor is the reason taking such a name, in that case, ticularly clear; and, what seems conclusive against it, the name many years before the alleged date tragic event. The church lately lished was built in the reign of Charles upon the site of a more ancient stru The new church, which is to be thirteenth-century Gothic style, red brick with stone dressings, has designed by Mr. E. C. Lee, architect Bedford-row. The memorial stone laid by Mr. O. Coope, M.P., on Tue last, in the presence of the Bish London, and of more than a the spectators. The Lord Mayor, be tained by official duties in the City requested the Rev. James Cohen, president of the building committee late Rector of Whitechapel, to pres his absence.

The proceedings commenced be

St Mary Matfelon, Whitechapel. *Illustrated London News*

The remains
of St Leonard's
Priory. *Robert
Wynn Jones,
lostcityoflondon.
co.uk*

THE FIRST EAST END CELEBRITY

This had to be Geoffrey Chaucer, who lived in rooms over
the gate at Aldgate from 1374 to be near to his work as
Commissioner of Customs in the Port of London. It is likely
that the accommodation was funded by John of Gaunt,
although Chaucer's wealthy father (a vintner) had land,
shops, gardens and even a brewery in the vicinity. Chaucer
lived there for twelve years, a period during which many
of his poems were written and where he started writing
The Canterbury Tales. There is a reference to the convent
at Stratford-atte-Bow (St Leonard's) in this famous book,
the prioress having studied French there, which she 'spak ful
faire and fetisly'.

The area would have been busy, the building astride a
muddy highway into London, a caretaker employed to
keep the road under the gate in good repair, and with tolls
charged from 1376, but this does not seem to have damaged Chaucer's creativity. Fourteenth-century threats of

invasion from the French may have worried him, however, following the death of Edward III, because by 1377 there were ordinances in place to fortify the gate with portcullises, and residents were told to be ready to defend the city.

THE BRIGHT SIDE: FAIRS AND FUN

A grant was made by Henry III in 1229 to celebrate Pentecost (now known as Whit Sunday) for fifteen days annually in East Smithfield (and elsewhere). Henry IV continued with a further grant of the right of a fair within the grounds of St Katharine's Hospital, again in East Smithfield, to last twenty-one days from the Feast of St James in July, to help with fundraising. The first of these took place in 1442 and continued for over a century, but it is not clear how long the Pentecost fair lasted.

Hunting had been popular in the wood owned by the Bishop of London (later the area that became Victoria Park), rendering the bishop unpopular when he attempted to enclose it for his own private parties and provoking a mass protest in 1292. It seemed the locals won a victory after submitting a petition to the king and could continue chasing rabbits, hares and foxes. Incidentally, hunting dogs (greyhounds?) were alleged to have been kept on the Isle of Dogs by Edward III, but this could well have been a legend to account for the area's name! What is more factual is the annual feast that was held in the bishop's woods on May Day, attended by the aldermen and sheriffs of the city.

It appears that there were tournaments held near to Stepney Manor House in the fourteenth century, involving armoured horsemen, although probably pre-dating jousting. The Stepney Roll of 1308, published in the nineteenth

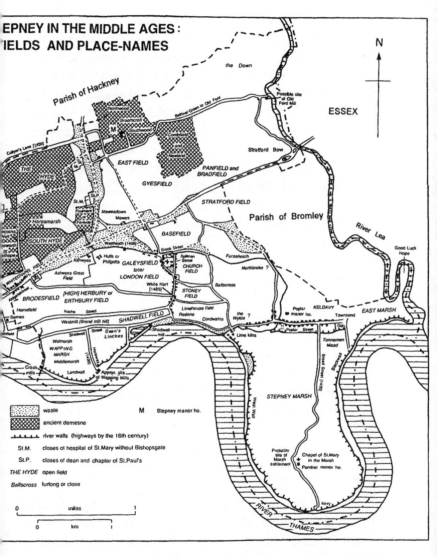

Map of Stepney in the Middle Ages. *British History Online (BHO), Institute of Historical Research*

century as *Collectanea Topographica et Genealogica*, gives a list of the knights present at one particular event. One specialist website even mentions the king (Edward II) attending a tournament here in 1309, which seems a distinct possibility especially allowing for the fact that his 1308 coronation was apparently celebrated here in some style. Confusingly, some sources suggest that this celebratory tournament was cancelled by Edward, fearful of his favourite, Piers Gaveston, being assaulted. At the 1309 tournament, one illustrious knight, Giles Argentine, was apparently proclaimed King of the Greenwood. According to the anonymous 1309 chronicle *Annales Londonienses*, Giles was a reckless chap, a kind of fourteenth-century naughty-but-nice outlaw. The location continued to be popular for such events, because Edward III also attended one here in 1330.

For a taste of something different, the public were allowed to view an elephant, an exotic gift presented to King Henry III by King Louis IX in 1255. It could be seen within the confines of the Tower of London, being part of the menagerie started by King John in 1210 which included a lion, leopards and a polar bear.

THE DARK SIDE: PLAGUES AND LEPERS

The plague reached London in 1348, and King Edward III closed a number of the larger ports to try and confine its spread. The numbers known to have died in the city are not proven, but are estimated to have been between a third and a half of the population, i.e. up to 30,000 of its 70,000 residents. Locally, the East Smithfield cemetery was established as the prime burial ground for plague victims, rather than filling the local churchyards. In 1348 and 1349 Court Rolls were issued, listing the dead, revealing that more than a third of Stepney's peasants had lost their lives between 1348 and 1349, whole families being decimated. When the cemetery was excavated in the 1980s, experts suggested that burials of up to 200 people per day had taken place at one point. In Stepney, the highest estimated death toll in one month was seventy-five for February 1349, according to the manorial court records – although these courts, held in Stepney (presumably at a local manor house) from 1228 onwards, were primarily for landlords to make decisions with regard to the claims and complaints of tenants.

The *East End Chronicles* has a fascinating story of a group of 120 holy men, sent by Pope Clement VI to the East End in 1348 to walk the streets 'chanting paternosters and Ave Marias' as an antidote to the plague. At Stepney Green it seems they stopped, stripped to the waist and passed around 'heavy leather scourges tipped with metal studs' which were used to beat each other 'until the blood flowed freely' – a ceremony repeated three times a day for the next month. Did this help? It seems unlikely …

When leprosy became widespread during the eleventh century, one of the ten isolation hospitals in the London area was located at Mile End. The disease was thought to be contagious and the sufferers were banned from public places including churches, and had to cover themselves and to ring a bell to warn of their presence. There was another such hospital on the Hackney border.

Edward III founded a monastery on the site of the East Smithfield burial ground *c.* 1353 – St Mary Graces, also known as the New Abbey or Eastminster – for Roman Catholic Cistercian monks and also to commemorate the Black Death. Another health measure initiated by the crown was that all meat should be killed and cleaned outside the confines of the city (e.g. in the area of St Leonard's, Bromley-by-Bow) although it could be sold within its boundaries, with butchers being fined or imprisoned if they broke the rule. In 1362 there were celebrations as plague deaths came to an end, although the plague was to reappear at intervals for several centuries. The resultant labour shortage, incidentally, afforded women more opportunities and increased their social standing, and forced up wages for both men and women – so good news for some.

THE WATERY SIDE

Soon after its founding, the responsibility of maintaining the dykes and preventing breaches in the river walls was passed to the monastery of St Mary Graces, a responsibility they could have done without given the East End's track record when it came to flooding. There were floods in Wapping in 1323 and in Stepney in 1369, and the most devastating flood – with the loss of many lives and destroying property and cattle – followed in 1448. This is when the Thames burst its banks and covered much of Stepney and Poplar, with the Isle of Dogs particularly badly hit, leaving it desolate, with only fish and fishermen remaining. In fact, the eastern edge of the Isle of Dogs remained the preferred area for fishing because the trade was not hindered by ships anchored offshore.

Trade was, however, hindered when the Thames froze over in 1410 and again in 1434. Such bitter temperatures not only interrupted supplies but also threatened livestock.

MORE MONKS AND NUNS

The East End highways and byways must have seen quite a lot of religious figures during the Middle Ages, given the number of abbeys and monasteries within its confines. Apart from Eastminster, a priory which became the Royal Hospital of Bethlem (or Bedlam) was built in 1247 on land donated outside the city walls in Stepney by Simon Fitzmary, a wealthy city merchant. The monks of St Mary of Bethlem initially focused on the shelter and care of the homeless, but gradually began to focus on those with mental illnesses; the hospital later became notorious for its callous treatment of those in its 'care'. Patients rarely stayed more than a year and were then licensed to beg on main routes.

Additionally, the Abbey of St Clare was established in Aldgate some time before 1293 by Edward I's brother Edmund, Earl of Lancaster, becoming known as the House of Minoresses. Edward's sister-in-law brought the first Franciscan nuns, or Poor Clares, to England from Europe. Financially, the abbey benefited from aristocratic female patronage, and it was also granted privileges by the king and the pope (e.g. no taxation!) and endowed with land and paying tenants. The convent also seems to have run a farm producing income and food. Some high-status women became residents – Margaret Beauchamp, the widow of the Earl of Warwick, was granted leave by the pope to reside in the house from 1401, and Lady Scrope took the veil there after being widowed. The abbey attracted the daughters and widows of the wealthy. Patrons buried here included the Countess of Clare, founder of Clare College Cambridge (1360), and the Duchess of York, Anne Mowbray, child-bride of one of the murdered princes in the Tower (1481).

The priory or hospital of the Blessed Virgin Mary without Bishopsgate, later called St Mary Spital, was built on land donated by wealthy merchants in what is now Spitalfields, on the site of a Roman cemetery; such gifts by the wealthy were regarded as a route to heaven rather than hell. Its foundations were laid in 1197, and it was partly rebuilt and extended in later years, comprising infirmaries, private rooms and gardens for the canons and the lay sisters who looked after the sick, barns, kitchens, at least one private well, and orchards and stables. The building was occupied by canons and lay brothers and sisters of the Augustinian order but one of its principal features initially was to serve as a lying-in hospital (a maternity unit, as we would call it now), looking after both mothers and their children. In the fourteenth century, royal servants and local landowners were among the patients. All that remains since the closing of the monasteries in London is the charnel house, built in

Remains of the Charnel House, St Mary Spital. *Richard Nevell, via commons.wikimedia.org/wiki*

1320, where bones disturbed during grave-digging were stored. Close to this site were the oldest buildings in the area now known as Shoreditch, but the whole area was relatively rural during the Middle Ages.

KEEPING WELL AND WATERED

Not just another monk (well, a Dominican friar) was Henry Daniel, who achieved a level of fame as a fourteenth-century medic, horticulturalist and writer. He had extensive gardens in Stepney, listing over 250 different plants, providing herbs for medical use. Within his many manuscripts – written in English and Latin, and preserved at the Bodleian Library – he writes of treating the nobility, and at least one plant in his garden came from the garden of Queen Philippa, Edward III's wife.

For East Enders wanting a different route to oblivion, the first hostelries began to appear. The only one where there appears to be confirmed fifteenth-century roots (1460s) is the Town of Ramsgate, still beside the Thames at Wapping. It is now Grade II listed but started as just the Hostel, then the Red Cow (after a red-headed barmaid!) and the Prince of Denmark before ending up as the Town of Ramsgate. The name is attributed to the many Ramsgate fishermen who unloaded their catch at Wapping Old Stairs rather than pay the taxes involved if they travelled further into London.

EAST END MANSIONS

Not a contradiction in terms! The site of the London Chest Hospital in Bethnal Green was the original location for Stepney Manor House, the property of the Bishop of London from the beginning of the thirteenth century. As lord of the manor the bishop would use it for himself or part of his household. The house had its own chapel, stables, dovecot and kitchen gardens. At the edge of the bishop's woods (which evolved into Victoria Park) there was said to have been a castle near the River Lea at Old Ford associated with King John, although there is no evidence that he visited, rendering the association unclear. However, the then Duke of Gloucester does seem to have had links with the area. This castle seems to have been the stuff of legend, and has often been confused with the 'palace' at Stepney, which started life as King John's Palace.

Based more on legend than fact is the story linked to a mansion known as Montford House in what is now Victoria Park Square in Bethnal Green. This was described as a crenellated red brick building (by Jane Cox, in *London's East End Life and Traditions*) and owned by Henry de Montfort, who was allegedly blinded at the Battle of Evesham (1265). The story

goes that he would only give his daughter's hand in marriage to someone who would approach him for her hand when he was dressed as a beggar, i.e. someone not after her inheritance. When one of Bessie's many admirers was indeed willing to approach what appeared to be a 'blind beggar' he is said to have given not only his permission but a £3,000 dowry plus funding for a wedding dress

The Blind Beggar, as per the pub sign. *Author's collection* to the tune of £100. Impressive. The legend has lingered over the centuries and is commemorated in the Stepney pub, the Blind Beggar, but the house itself looks to have been built at a far later period of history and the general consensus is that both Henry de Montfort and his father, Simon, were killed (Henry's body being mutilated) at the battle.

In 1299, Edward I summoned members of parliament to meet at the Lord Mayor of London's house near St Dunstan's Church. This was the residence of Henry Le Waley, a wealthy vintner, and was described as the 'Great Place', where the statute was issued to stop imitation coins being imported and English coins exported. Just a few years earlier, there are reports of Edward staying at the 'Shadwell manor house' of the Dean and Chapter of St Paul's. Later Lord Mayors had houses, variously, in Poplar and Mile End.

There was also a Cobham's Manor, near Whitechapel church, owned by a rich lawyer, Thomas Morice, who died in 1368. Then there was Poplar Manor House, one of several owned by the Abbot of Tower Hill, and home of the Poultney family in the fourteenth century, where the Black Prince, son of Edward III, reputedly stayed when courting his future wife, whose family lived in a similar Poplar mansion.

Stepney certainly seemed to be attracting the aristocracy as well as merchants; while little is known of their actual dwellings, records show that Thomas Holland, Earl of Kent, had a sizeable estate in Stepney in the fourteenth century, as did John Howard, Duke of Norfolk, 100 years later. South of St Dunstan's was another 'great place' owned by Henry Colet, a wealthy cloth merchant, in the fifteenth century. The area was obviously becoming popular with those who possessed money and status, Londoners who wanted gardens and orchards within a half hour of the city by river or horse.

EARNING DOSH

As the population of London grew, so did the demand for bread, meaning that those working in the East End mills and bakehouses during this period were busy, and profitable. There were at least five mills by 1233 in and around Wapping and Shadwell, with more on the Thames near East Smithfield and Aldgate (the latter owned by the Priory of Holy Trinity). A fulling mill, improving on the texture of woven cloth, was operational in Old Ford on the Lea by the end of the thirteenth century, but other local watermills were also being adapted, giving the area, and its residents, another income. Wool was an important commodity nationally, although there were not too many sheep on Stepney marshes. Nevertheless there are records of heathland used as pasture for sheep in Bethnal Green (the area now known as Cambridge Heath). Cloth, however, was at the epicentre of foreign exports, and, in return, wine, fruit, spices and glassware were now being imported. Corn mills did continue to outnumber fulling mills in the area, however.

As trade grew, locally and internationally, the East End was not just producing bread and cloth. The famous bell foundry of Whitechapel started out in Aldgate by the middle of the thirteenth century, by which time there were breweries, tanners, blacksmiths, potters and butchers in that area. There were, of course, still peasants digging ditches and threshing corn. By the middle of the fourteenth century there was a thriving trade in crossbows, arrows, armour and cannon with workshops also at Aldgate and near the Tower.

There was also the start of shipbuilding activity in Ratcliff with wharves and warehouses being constructed around

Ratcliff Ferry. *Anonymous print from Wonderful London (London, 1926)*

Wapping from 1395 onwards. The historian Dr Kevin McDonnell gives evidence (slender, but convincing) of ships and barges being built for Edward III at Ratcliff because it was 'close to London', had river access 'not impeded by marsh' and was also close to the timber supply provided by the 'Middlesex woods' (see *Medieval London Suburbs*). The area around Limehouse and Ratcliff was a natural location as a landing spot, and industries such as rope-making were developed in the area. Watermen could charge passengers who wanted transport into London, and an early ferry seems to have been in use by the end of the fourteenth century between the Isle of Dogs and Greenwich.

Life was not easy for medieval tradesmen, wherever they lived, with restrictions on prices, on weight (of bread, for example), of quality (e.g. shoe leather), and palatability (e.g. meat and fish). Offending butchers or fishmongers would be subject to the pillory, with their potentially poisonous foodstuffs set on fire beneath them.

As London's population grew – including East London, with some 4,000 residents by the middle of the fourteenth century – the building trade was particularly busy with the advent of brickmakers, glaziers, carpenters and stonemasons. Chalk arrived by river from Kent into the kilns of Stepney, producing the lime that was needed in the production of the necessary mortar, hence Limehouse of course, and the kiln owners would have been the equivalent of today's millionaires.

Quite a few women were making money as madams, with brothels and prostitutes abounding around the Whitechapel and East Smithfield areas. Many prostitutes were Dutch, and they ran the risk of fines or of the humiliating pillory. There was actually a dress code for prostitutes in the fourteenth century – red-and-white-striped hoods – to distinguish them from the respectable! Punishment for common whores was likely to have been an embarrassing ride in a cart with matching red-and-white-striped awning to a thew (pillory for women) such as the one at Aldgate, where their hair would be cut. The Dutch, incidentally, seemed to have been at the forefront of the growth in gambling at the time. They could probably not be blamed, however, for the increase in syphilis from the end of the fifteenth century, resulting in the closure of a number of brothels in areas like Shoreditch, West Smithfield and St Katherine's, which promptly reopened when the women had been medically checked.

AND TALKING OF MAKING MONEY...

In 1279 the Royal Mint was formed within the Tower of London. As a fortress, it was the ideal, secure location for producing the country's coins, right down to the silver groat (four old pence) impressed with the head of Edward I, who was on the throne when it was introduced. It survived in the Tower in what seems to have been rather cramped conditions for the next 500 years.

ENDING WITH SOME ROYALS IN THE EAST END

When Edward II's widow, Isabella, the 'she-wolf of France' died in 1358, her funeral procession passed through Essex from Castle Rising in Norfolk with an overnight rest at Mile End before her burial service in London. According to research by Kathryn Warner (in *Isabella of France: The Rebel Queen*), John Galeys, the owner of the house where the cortege stayed, was paid £10 for his services.

A hundred years later, during the Wars of the Roses, Edward IV married Elizabeth Woodville (a commoner and a Lancastrian, while the ruling nobility were Yorkists), but when he died in 1483, the throne was seized from their son Edward V. Both he and Elizabeth's younger son were declared illegitimate (for convoluted reasons) and hidden away in the Tower. Just months later, Elizabeth's brother-in-law, their legal 'Protector', was crowned Richard III (the last king of the House of York and the last Plantagenet ruler), and the two boys were never seen again, presumably murdered – a source of ongoing conjecture.

And so began a new era: the age of the Tudors.

5

TUDORS

THE DISAPPEARING PEASANT

As the centuries passed, East End parishioners earned a living in more urban ways. The peasants who had farmed the land, fished the rivers and cut the trees gave way to craftsmen (and women) and traders and mariners. They were beginning to specialise and not just in domestic trades such as bread-making and beer-brewing, but in dyeing cloth, making tiles, woodworking and metalworking: developing real, profitable skills. One particularly successful local was John Gardiner (d. 1599), who lived on Mile End Green and who owned the Ratcliff Sugar Company, processing West Indian cane near where Cable Street is now.

The growth in the maritime industries along the riverbanks and the influx of immigrants from Europe in the sixteenth century impacted to a large extent on the East End. Although 30,000 people living in 7 square miles is not overcrowded by today's standards, this nevertheless meant that Tower Hamlets was expanding fast. The Dutch and Flemish fled the invading Spaniards in 1567, and five years later the French Protestant Huguenots fled the Catholics following their massacre in Paris on St Bartholomew's Day, prompting a religious civil war. Thousands of immigrants settled in Aldgate, Shoreditch, St Katharine's, East Smithfield, Poplar, Stepney and Bethnal Green.

Dutch and Flemish names begin to turn up in records of burgeoning industries – brewing and armament making around Whitechapel, and an army of people employed in Aldgate, East Smithfield and Old Ford making the fine clothes now being demanded. Anyone with land was finding it more profitable for brick-making than agriculture – in Whitechapel, for instance. A bell foundry in Houndsditch, now that there was less demand for bells following the religious changes, turned to making cannons, but the making of bells continued with the establishment of the world's oldest manufacturing company, the Whitechapel Bell Foundry, responsible in later years for Big Ben. It dates from at least 1570 and quite possibly even earlier, and continued in business until finally closing in 2016. During Edward VI's short reign (1547–53), the Middlesex county records show that around one fifth of the county's alehouses were in Stepney and Whitechapel, spawning the growth of a substantial brewing industry in the East End.

Nearly all the gunners employed in England in the sixteenth century were from western Europe, such as Anthony Anthony (Dutch) an armourer in East Smithfield, near the Tower, and Peter Bawde (or Bawood: French) who headed up a foundry in Houndsditch, close by.

CREATING RECREATION

Sixteenth-century maps of the expanding London reveal not only the open spaces and fields in the East End but some of the activities taking place there. The engraved copper plate at the Museum of London dating from 1559 which depicts

Whitechapel Bell Foundry. *Maggie Jones, via Flickr*

the Moorfields area as shown on one of the earliest maps of the location, for instance, shows cattle and horses grazing close to the city gates, archers practising at Spitalfields, gardens and fountains in Shoreditch. It was the Spitalfields area that sported the Artillery Ground, appointed by King Henry VIII as such for weaponry practice. This usage lives on in street names such as Gun Street and Artillery Lane. Archery practice was thought of as a form of civil defence, and it took place in several other local areas – Finsbury Fields and Hoxton Fields, for example. The latter was also used to settle quarrels by duelling. Ben Jonson (the dramatist who was Shakespeare's competition at the time) killed the actor Gabriel Spencer in 1598 as a result of one such duel.

Archery was favoured by royalty, but property owners in Shoreditch and Hoxton were less keen on the hazard of flying arrows and so built hedges and ditches to cause inconvenience to the practising archers and gunmen early in the sixteenth century. However, the young sportsmen banded together in number to destroy these obstacles. Not always successfully, as Thomas Downs wrote in the *East End Local Advertiser* on 16 August 1902 of an incident in 1579 when a bystander was 'struck on the head by an arrow shot by John Savadge, late of Stebunbeth (Stepney), yeoman, and received a wound from which he died on the 3rd of September'.

John Stow writes in his 1598 *Survay* [*sic*] *of London* that the area now known as Petticoat Lane was a place of elm trees and pleasant fields, for citizens to 'walk, shoot … and refresh their dull spirits in the sweet and wholesome air'. He also refers to fields being turned into gardens, such as one belonging to the Priory of Holy Trinity which began growing 'herbs and roots' for market. Nearby, at Goodman's Fields, Aldgate (the land then owned by the Minoresses of St Clare), was where he collected his daily milk.

Mile End Green was the site of a mock battle between the English and Spanish in July 1588 when Philip II's Armada was preparing to invade – watched by a very patriotic crowd. It seems to have been a popular venue during Tudor times, for 'halberdiers, arquebusiers … City bands… [serving as] a camp of exercise … [and for] medieval gymkhana[s]', according to Charles McNaught in the *East London Advertiser* of 30 October 1909. A halberd was a form of battleaxe and an arquebus was a portable gun. Mile End Green was already known by then as a location for military training.

The East End was at the forefront of early theatre performances, partly because the authorities refused to allow plays within the city walls. Before 1574, plays were performed by touring players in the yards of a flurry of newly

Shakespeare. *Motif collection*

built inns, but when these activities started being regulated, purpose-built wooden theatres appeared. The Red Lion Theatre was built in the garden of a farm-house in Mile End in 1567 at a cost of £20, which included trapdoors, gal-leries, a turret and a fixed stage; it only seems to have survived for one summer season, the winter making it tricky to access across open farmland, perhaps. The man behind it, grocer John Brayne, then collaborated with actor-manager James Burbage to build The Theatre at Shoreditch in 1576 (off Curtain Road), moving away from touring groups to repertory. The name 'Theatre' was chosen because of its Roman antecedents, and the venue – which cost well in excess of £200 – staged the first Shakespeare plays. Performances were held in the afternoons (because there was no artificial lighting or heating) until the building was demolished in 1598 following a number of legal disputes with the landlord; the timbers and tiles were used to build the famous Globe across the river. The Curtain opened nearby just a year after The Theatre, with Shakespeare's company – no doubt including the Bard himself – playing regularly at both venues. *Romeo and Juliet* is said to have had its first staging at the Curtain in 1598.

John Wolfe, a successful East Smithfield publisher, attempted to build another theatre in what is now Thomas More Street (near St Katherine Docks) but although work started on construction it never opened. This was in part due to the fact that theatre had an unsavoury reputation, with women who attended often wearing masks to disguise their identity: there were no women on stage, of course. Another East End venue was the Boar's Head in Whitechapel, which started with performances in the inn yard from 1557, progressing to open-air amphitheatre status in 1599. During its first season, it became temporarily famous when the Lord Mayor of London intervened to stop what was regarded as a lewd play being performed resulting in the arrest of the players – *A Sackful of News*, by an unknown playwright, which apparently attacked the establishment.

If cream and cakes was more appealing as a recreation, then 'Stratford Bow' was recommended by William Kemp, Shakespeare's comic actor, when he danced his way to Norwich, via Mile End, in 1599. For alcohol, there are a couple of pubs still in the East End that date from the sixteenth century, the rest (and there were certainly many) long gone – the Grapes (formerly Bunch of Grapes) in Narrow Street, Limehouse, dates from 1583. (It is now owned by no less a personage than Sir Ian McKellen!)

The Prospect of Whitby in Wapping dates from around 1520, laying claim to being the oldest riverside pub on the Thames, having had several earlier names (a similar claim to the Town of Ramsgate, as we saw in Chapter Four).

THE UPMARKET EAST END

Sixteenth-century maps show large dwellings in Stepney, Spitalfields, Shoreditch and Whitechapel, surrounded by open spaces, the kind of dwellings that were attracting those wanting a 'country' retreat. Following on from the grand houses being built in the fifteenth century was a large, whitewashed, timber-framed mansion in Bethnal Green, rebuilt on the site of an earlier dwelling for John Kirby, a wealthy Elizabethan merchant. This dates from 1570, originally Bethnal or (Bednall) House, but becoming known as Kirby's Castle, occupying the site of what became Bethnal Green Library. When the lawyer and scientist Sir Hugh Platt occupied the house at the end of the sixteenth century, he wrote books about gardening and tobacco-growing, and about his experiments making wine with grapes grown in Bethnal Green. His fame was such that even Sir Francis Drake was said to have visited him to see how meat could be preserved and water kept drinkable. Platt also published a book called *Delights for Ladies*, detailing housewifely arts including preserving fruit and beauty 'aids', which remained in print until 1948!

Kirby's Castle, Bethnal Green. *From Walter Thorbury, Old and New London (London, 1878)*

Dating back even earlier – to 1490, i.e. the early Tudor period – is Bromley Hall in Bow, seemingly the oldest brick-built house in London. It was built by Holy Trinity Priory on the foundations of an even older manor house. This building was seized in 1531 during the Dissolution of the Monasteries and was then refurbished by Henry VIII, ostensibly for personal use while hunting. However, it was occupied by the father of Elizabeth Blount, one of Henry's young mistresses, and one who bore him a son he acknowledged as his: Henry Fitzroy, *c.* 1519. Thus it seems there were other reasons for Henry's involvement. John Blount died the year Henry's refurbishing started; the house gained rich tapestries, carvings and artwork, with no expense spared.

Worcester House in Stepney Green was the home of the Marquis of Worcester from 1597, a large moated mansion with a crenellated gatehouse, once known as the Great Place. This level of status would have meant that the house kept servants, footmen and grooms. This is probably the house once known as King John's Palace, having been rebuilt and renamed over the centuries. Excavations of the area during the Crossrail dig in 2011 revealed the remains of several further large buildings occupying the area. Around Worcester House itself information about the inhabitants' diet became evident, with findings of fruit stones and pips from figs, plums, cherries and apples, remains of marrow and pumpkin, and pieces of walnut and hazelnut shells. In 1516 the house was leased to Lord Darcy, executed in 1537 at Tower Hill for his part in the rebellion against Henry VIII's Dissolution of the Monasteries (this revolt was called the Pilgrimage of Grace). This was in fact quite a fall from 'grace' as Darcy had been appointed to search for and interrogate suspected persons, e.g. courtiers, with information useful in Anne Boleyn's trial. Sir John Neville,

King John's Palace. *Illustrated London News*

who had a substantial residence on the south side of the Mile End Road, had headed up this 'Pilgrimage' – another trusted aristocrat, he too was executed for treason in 1541.

Near St Dunstan's was another grand house where Sir Henry Colet lived until his death in 1505, with Thomas Cromwell taking up a fifty-year lease there from 1533, his principal seat as he rose to power and eventually sent his neighbour Darcy to the gallows. This was apparently a traditional, timbered courtyard house, and was also known intermittently, and confusingly, as the Great Place or Mercers' Great Place, Colet having been a leading member of the Mercers' Company. Nearby, his only surviving son (of twenty-two children), John, had a similarly large house set among orchards on the corner of what is now Salmon Lane (some historians think it was the same house). He was the man who became Dean of St Paul's and entertained leading European thinkers in this house, including Erasmus, who wrote to him of Stepney being a place of 'rural peace ... a pleasant prospect ... [with] bounteous gifts of nature'. Another visitor and friend was Sir Thomas More, who would have arrived by boat at Ratcliff Stairs from his Chelsea home, and who wrote similarly of Stepney's 'delights'. When the dean founded St Paul's School, he gifted the house to the head-master as a country residence.

A few miles north, in Hoxton on the Shoreditch borders, the village settlement grew as courtiers and foreign ambas-sadors built large houses convenient for London, and yet surrounded by countryside. The Portuguese ambassa-dor had a house here from 1568 with a private chapel for English Catholics, forbidden in local churches now that Elizabeth I was on the throne. This breach of the new law actually brought out the parish constables, but they were chased away by the ambassador and his guests waving their swords! Some of the houses built in this area have been described as having 'towers, turrets and chimney tops not so much for use ... as for show and pleasure' (see the *Record of St Giles Cripplegate*, 1688, by Rev. W. Denton). A musician at the court of Elizabeth I, Jerome Bassano, used his accumulated wealth to buy a house in Hoxton Street *c.*1589, but was robbed nine years later of gold, jewellery and cash amounting to £120 – the equivalent of some £25,000 in modern terms, such being the status of the local residents.

The rich Throckmorton family had more than one property in the East End, but the one at Mile End was particularly lavish, described as having fourteen servants including one black slave, and sporting Turkish carpets. Arthur Throckmorton had married one of the queen's ladies-in-waiting, and his sister Bess, another lady-in-waiting, had married Sir Walter Raleigh when pregnant; Elizabeth disapproved of such marriages by her ladies. Bess tried to keep the pregnancy secret by moving in with her brother in Mile End for the confinement in 1592 but was soon arrested and sent, apparently with her baby, to the Tower, Sir Walter joining her weeks later. Both were eventually released, the baby having died in the meantime from the plague, although Raleigh was to upset the queen yet again and spend even more time in the Tower.

It was not only Arthur Throckmorton who could boast of having a black slave during this period. The Guildhall Library Manuscript Section gives parish register entries for a number of East End churches, with long lists of burials and baptisms of servants and slaves described mainly as 'blackamoors' (variety of spellings). To look at just one church, St Botolph's at Aldgate, there are eight such burials listed between 1586 and 1597. Half of these died from the plague, not unexpectedly, and their employers are given as mainly local merchants and brewers from in and around East Smithfield. A 1597 baptism is particularly interesting as it relates to a Mary Fillis, a 'blackmore' servant to a female 'seamster' in East Smithfield and the daughter of a 'basket maker' and 'shovel maker' named rather exotically as 'Fillis of Morisco' (Morisco is Spanish for 'Little Moor'). The area's multi-ethnicity is obviously nothing new – note that Henry VIII had a black drummer.

AND A BIT MORE DOWNMARKET

John Stow conjures up a different image – regarding the Wapping area, at least – of an East End drained early on in the sixteenth century, with houses built along the river embankment, partly to secure the land against floods. He described the riverside as a 'filthy straight passage, with alleys of small tenements ... inhabited by sailors' victuallers'. Certainly this area would have been crowded with ships' workshops and lodging houses for sailors, although, to be fair, this also became home to naval commanders of some distinction including Sir William Burrough (spellings vary), one-time Comptroller of the Queen's Navy in the sixteenth century, and the explorer Sir Humphrey Gilbert. Even Sir Walter Raleigh was reputed to have lived close by Blackwall Stairs at some point, though this is disputed. It is true that his letters, often mentioned by historians, regularly refer to the area, although he could of course just have been a frequent visitor. There are a number of references to Blackwall, Ratcliff and Mile End, variously spelled, in these letters, which can be viewed in the University of California Library archive online. More convincing is historian Charles McNaught – a frequent contributor to the *East London Observer* in the early twentieth century – who points out that the 'burial of a manservant of Sir Walter Raylie' was recorded in the register of Stepney Church on 25 August 1596; McNaught was convinced that Raleigh lived on Mile End Green. Interestingly, one local history website estimates that almost half of the 2,000 people who lived in Limehouse by the time of Elizabeth I's death (1603) 'had some seafaring connection' (www.eastlondonhistory.co.uk).

Another John – John Strype – wrote an updated version of Stow's *Survay* [*sic*] in 1720. He wrote of the 'poorer sorts of trades' moving to London in Elizabethan times, with the traders forced to operate outside the city walls because of the restrictions. These traders apparently made 'counterfeit' indigo, musk, saffron, cochineal, nutmeg, wax and even steel, although Strype describes them as 'bunglers'. His predecessor had already written of how slum housing was intruding on common land, especially on Whitechapel Road, leading out of Aldgate, but this area was outside the control of the authorities. Aldgate itself was losing its profusion of gardens and allotments by the end of the sixteenth century, giving way to industry.

The *East London Advertiser* of 23 August 1902 gives an account of the unsavoury nature of Shoreditch in 1595 by 'A writer', who says that, 'I commend our unclean sisters in Shoreditch … to the protection of … the Devil, hoping that you will speedily carry them to hell, there to keep open house … and not to let our ayre [*sic*] be contaminated with their sixpenny damnation any longer.'

EVEN NASTIER

The worst bout of bubonic plague (the most common form of what became known as the Black Death) in the sixteenth century was in 1563, when nearly a quarter of London's population died. In 1518 the first regulations were introduced in London: a bale of straw had to be hung on a pole outside infected houses for forty days and anyone from an infected home had to carry a white stick when they went out, to warn others to stay away. Carried by rodents, the plague spread less effectively in rural areas, but Spitalfields was particularly badly hit.

When Henry VIII split with the Roman Catholic Church (enabling him to marry Anne Boleyn) he started a turbulent period of change, which continued after his death. There followed two brief stints on the throne: his son Edward VI, and Lady Jane Grey. Making much more of an impression was Mary I, who, on becoming queen in 1553, now pursued the Protestants in her famously bloody fashion, and imprisoned the young Elizabeth, her own half-sister, at the Tower in 1554. When Elizabeth became queen following Mary's death (allegedly of cancer) she reversed the whole national culture, persecuting the Catholics (while, in her case, establishing a settled monarchy). One example was local man Thomas

Tresham from Hoxton, imprisoned in the Fleet Prison in 1581 for harbouring Edmund Campion, a Catholic priest. Campion was executed and Thomas spent several years after his release under house arrest at another house in Hoxton, which he regarded as noisy, with unsavoury residents.

Henry VIII. *Motif collection*

However, Mary's reign had a particular impact on the East End, a stopping-off place for her in August 1553 (at Mile End and at Whitechapel and Aldgate) en route to her coronation at Westminster Abbey via the Tower of London. While this brought out the crowds, it was the actions which soon followed that had a devastating effect, with bonfires burning heretics in Smithfield and in what is now Bow. Some 300 Protestants were executed between February 1555 and November 1558, so many that an execution site was set up in Bow (then Stratford-atte-Bow or Stratford-le-Bow). A particularly memorable day was 27 June 1556, when thirteen prisoners from Newgate prison in London were tied to three stakes and burned at the Bow site, watched by a crowd of 20,000. These were ordinary working folk – men and women – with strong religious convictions for which they were prepared to lose their lives. Elizabeth's reign became gradually more settled, and in the East End it was mainly the churches that were affected – organs were removed, as were any 'popish' ornaments. All the convents and priories in

Tower Hamlets had already been closed and their wealth confiscated during the reign of Henry VIII, excepting the Royal 'Hospital' of St Katherine, which was initially under the protection of three consecutive queen consorts.

By the beginning of the sixteenth century, the Execution Dock at Wapping was established. This was where those condemned by the High Court of Admiralty were hanged, usually arriving by cart from Marshalsea prison. Although it became famous as the place to execute pirates, most unfortunates were in fact murderers and thieves, though with an emphasis on crime at sea; land-based crime was more likely to result in execution at Tyburn in London. There was one bumper day on 10 August 1583, however, when a total of ten pirates were hanged at Execution Dock. A gibbet remains at the Prospect of Whitby pub nearby, but this is unlikely to have been the exact location, which has never really been securely evidenced, although there are stories about criminals being tied to posts in the nearby Thames and left to drown.

The Yeomen Warders at the Tower of London were formed in 1485 by Henry VII, and by the sixteenth century the law required the villages east of the Tower (i.e. Tower Hamlets) to provide the yeomen. In the meantime, the Tower had established a reputation as the foremost state prison in the country, from which no prisoner could escape. Many prisoners – especially noble ones like Sir Walter Raleigh, who spent over a decade here – were incarcerated, particularly when Henry VIII was on the throne. Lady Jane Grey and two of Henry's wives (Anne Boleyn and Catherine Howard) were executed away from the public eye on Tower Green in the sixteenth century, while many others, being less privileged in rank, like Thomas More, were executed outside the walls of the Tower, at Tower Hill.

For those without a trade, life was tough. It was a different life to those living in the grand houses – one with a short lifespan, a high child mortality rate and a growth in vagrancy, gambling and alcoholism. Brothels, particularly around East Smithfield, were busy, and Hog Lane market (later Rosemary Lane) did a flourishing trade in stolen goods. Certainly, there was quite a discrepancy between the rich and the poor, reminiscent perhaps of the twenty-first century. It wasn't until the reign of Elizabeth I that legislation was passed to address the needs of the poor, with the first Poor Law passed in 1601 to collect money from landowners to dispense to the local poor. By 1600 the East End had around 30,000 residents.

HELLO SAILOR

Some of those moving into the Stepney area would have been hoping to make a fortune in the New Worlds being discovered. Early explorer Sir Hugh Willoughby went in search of a route from Ratcliff to China in 1553, but only one of his three ships returned, and many East End crew were lost. Martin Frobisher attempted the same journey from Ratcliff (1576) and again from Blackwall (1577) with limited success. On one journey, he had taken six men whose death sentence had been commuted into banishment – they were landed on the shore of 'Freezeland' (probably today's Labrador) with weapons and provisions and instructions to win the goodwill and friendship of the natives. Frobisher became fascinated by the Eskimos on Baffin Island (Canada), bringing at least three back with him, none of whom survived. He also brought back what he believed to be gold, though it was proved worthless, but he had established the first overseas possession for Elizabeth I. There is plenty of evidence in historic journals and letters that Sir Walter Raleigh sailed from Limehouse on his voyage to Guinea on 14 October 1596.

Then there was Christopher Newport, who led nine expeditions from Limehouse to the West Indies, with one raid alone, in 1591, resulting in a cargo of livestock, tobacco, silks and merchandise worth an astounding £32,000. Sir Humphrey Gilbert (Walter Raleigh's half-brother) was a Limehouse resident for some years prior to 1578 and led an expedition to Newfoundland a few years later, securing it as the first overseas dominion of the crown, but losing his life on the homeward journey when his ship went down with all hands. Sir William Burrough lived in Limehouse in 1579, sailing several times to Russia followed by a further expedition resulting in the capture of ten pirates who were executed at Wapping (1583), and a voyage to Cadiz with Sir Francis Drake (1587). John Vassal of Ratcliff sent two ships, at his own expense, to fight the Armada in 1588, where Frobisher and Burrough also resurfaced, playing active roles. Sir Henry Palmer of Stepney was another local who featured in attacks on the Spanish fleet, as was William Coxe of Limehouse.

Spain was a real thorn in the flesh of local men, including Ratcliffe's William Mace who in 1589 had been persuaded, with his crew, to board a Spanish man-of-war to 'parley' but was subsequently attacked, few surviving (including Mace). He may have felt some compensation in his neighbour Robert Bradshaw's routing of five Spanish ships outside Gibraltar in 1591 and Thomas White's successful plundering of Spanish vessels a year later, the prizes being landed at Blackwall. Various accounts of these are available in the Guildhall Library, London.

6

STUARTS

UNHAPPY BEGINNINGS

The reign of James I kicked off, as far as the East End was concerned, with another bout of plague, seemingly brought over to its shore by ships from Europe. Overcrowding in the rapidly expanding areas bordering the river and the city walls led to its rapid spread, with thirty bodies a day being buried in Whitechapel alone and whole families being wiped out. Similar misfortune arrived following the coronation of Charles I (1625) with another serious outbreak, as if to remind the population that a new king did not mean their lives would improve. The charges for carts to carry dead bodies increased, the clergy were conducting funerals all day, and rosemary and frankincense were sprinkled in the streets in an attempt to disguise the stench. In 1665, not a coronation year this time (with Charles II now on the throne), there was yet another severe outbreak, described by Daniel Defoe in *Journal of the Plague Year* as raging in Aldgate and Whitechapel more so than anywhere else around London. Although Defoe was only 5 in 1665, he was probably right because by September there were red crosses on doors in every street, and more than ninety burials a day in Stepney alone, with large plague pits in Aldgate, Mile End and Bethnal Green filling up quickly, depopulating the area. Another explanation for the mysterious Whitechapel Mount, the site of the Royal London Hospital, was that debris from the Great Fire of London was heaped on top of a deep plague pit. There has been a lot of debate regarding the origins of the Mount, but no definitive answer.

At least the East End was 'safe' from this devastating fire, partly thanks to the east wind. In fact, it became a place of safety for those Londoners wanting to escape the devastation – people like Samuel Pepys, who took his valuables (and his diary) to his friend William Rider's house in Bethnal Green (Kirby's Castle: see Chapter Five). The area, devastated by the plague, was filling up again. The local sea captains and merchants would slowly be replaced in the East End churches by dock and factory workers.

LACKING IN POPULARITY

Returning to James I, he was the monarch at the centre of the Gunpowder Plot in 1605, of course. He had threatened to 'outlaw' all Roman Catholics, upsetting prominent Catholic families who had protected Jesuit priests during the reign of Elizabeth. The plotters planned to blow up the House of Lords during the State Opening of Parliament on 5 November 1605, but others, upset by the possibility of innocent victims, sent letters of warning to such luminaries as Lord Monteagle of Mile End Green – and he it was who took his letter to the authorities. Result: goodbye Guy Fawkes.

When James I stayed at the Tower from 1603, the last monarch to use it as a royal palace, he indulged in his favourite sport of baiting the lions with large mastiffs. While such a sport was not unusual, it seems particularly vicious. The reaction of East Enders is not recorded, as

Above left: Charles II. *Motif collection*

Above right: Samuel Pepys. *Author's cigarette card collection*

with Charles I chasing a stag from Wanstead to Wapping during a hunting expedition in 1629, killing the animal in Nightingale Lane. When Charles – a generally unpopular king thanks to his religious views and newly imposed taxes – was overthrown by Oliver Cromwell, it is said to be Richard Brandon, the hangman from Rosemary Lane, Whitechapel (now Royal Mint Street), who was his executioner. Brandon committed suicide soon after, in June 1649, and was buried in Whitechapel churchyard. There were also plenty of high-profile seventeenth-century executions at the Tower, statesman Thomas Wentworth, Archbishop William Laud, and the Duke of Monmouth among them.

Cromwell, while never a monarch of course, was unpopular for different reasons. His repressive Puritanical regime meant that the working people of the East End had to forfeit their excessive drinking and feasts, their parties and sports, with punishments for fornication and swearing and the death penalty for adultery; and rowdier pubs such as the Rose were closed down. The Civil War records reveal only minor clashes between Royalists and Roundheads in the East End, although no doubt some local men had been seduced by the idea of joining the New Model Army. One incident was in 1648 when 600 Royalist insurgents seized Bow Bridge (3 June) hoping that London would support the king, but they were turned away and forced to retreat over the River Lea into Essex. Cromwell did have one friend in Stepney, Maurice Thomson, a Puritan merchant who had made his money from American tobacco and was then living at the splendid Worcester House (see Chapter Five), which he sold in 1675 to the Church. It seems that the mysterious Whitechapel Mount may have been one of the fortifications built in 1642 to defend London against Royalist armies, although this is just one theory of its origins. Another fortification was built in Shoreditch just north of St Leonard's Church. Certainly there would have been disruption in other parts of the East End that were on the main route into London as defences were constructed against the Royalist threat.

While the East End was released from the yoke of Cromwell, with Charles II back on the throne in 1660, the restored king's attempt at religious toleration proved contentious, to put it mildly. He was a Protestant but with a Catholic mother and brother, remaining Protestant because this was the dominant religion in England. Local people treated Charles with suspicion, many going further with their outspoken dislike of the king's hedonistic lifestyle. East

Enders were hauled up in court for speaking out against the king, and men were arrested following riotous anti-government assemblies in Spitalfields, Whitechapel and Stepney. Religious meetings of more than five people were forbidden and this also meant that a number of East Enders were arrested for defying the law, especially Quakers. William Penn, friend and neighbour of Samuel Pepys, was imprisoned in the Tower in 1668 for seven months for publishing a pamphlet critical of the established church: as a Quaker, he had also attended meetings in a private house in Spitalfields. According to an article in the *East London Observer* of 25 March 1911, one Stepney Quaker, shoemaker James Otter, was sentenced to seven years' slavery in Virginia in 1664 for being 'a vagabond' as he refused to give an address, only that he dwelt 'in God'. Even the minister of Stepney Meeting House, Rev. Matthew Mead, living at Worcester House near St Dunstan's, was one of those complicit in a plan to murder Charles II and his brother in 1683 – called the Rye House Plot. He managed to escape by fleeing to Holland, but eventually returned to end his days back in Worcester House.

MORE REBELS

It was not just religion and the monarchy that provoked dissent in the East End in the seventeenth century – although the *Victoria County History of Middlesex* (Volume 11) reveals that more people from Stepney were arrested for religious dissent between 1661 and 1689 than in other local parishes. Additionally, in 1675 there was a large-scale protest by local silk weavers against the growth of multi-shuttle looms, which could do the work

Traditional loom. *Motif collection*

of twenty people, causing severe unemployment within their ranks. Mobs in Spitalfields, Stepney, Whitechapel, Shoreditch and Hoxton removed any looms they could find and burned them, with the local militia refusing to arrest them. However, once the Royal Guards were called upon, the ringleaders were arrested, pilloried and fined – and the multi-shuttle looms did not go away.

In 1668, Protestant dissenters were angry with Charles II because he was not tackling the growing prostitute 'problem', being apparently more concerned with cracking down on prayer meetings. As a result, the Bawdy House Riots, mainly involving young apprentices, ransacked the brothels of Wapping, Ratcliff, Stepney and Poplar as their way of protesting. Ironically, the most famous victim, Damaris Page, regarded Barbara Villiers (the Countess of Castlemaine), Charles II's mistress, as a contemporary sympathiser … see the section 'The Early Pen and Ink', below. Eight of these apprentices were executed.

East End coal heavers (who unloaded and moved coal from the ships on the Thames) were having their pay cut by agents who knew they had little choice in the matter (pre-trade unions), and were being overcharged at the inns run by many of the same 'agents'; they decided enough was enough in April 1691. They attacked one such agent,

John Green, at his tavern in Shadwell, which fronted the river. Green had been forewarned, and was ready with his servants, muskets and even a blunderbuss, holding off the mob until the military arrived. Seven rioters were hanged for their part in the disturbance.

AHOY THERE

Pirates were not only from Cornwall and other coastal towns. In the seventeenth century, the East End also had its share. John Mucknell, born in Stepney, was living in Poplar as a commander serving the East India Company's vessels. During the English Civil War he became known as the King's Pirate, siding with Charles I's Royalists against the fun-crushing Puritans, whom he regarded as 'roundhead devils' (see *The Pirate John Mucknell* by Todd Stevens). In 1644 he seized the brand new forty-four-gun ship under his command and used it to start another, less respectable, life as a pirate. Flying the king's flag, he is said to have 'inflicted terror' upon merchant shipping around the Isles of Scilly. His original ship, the *John*, had been shipwrecked in 1645. Mucknell escaped execution – he is thought to have died in 1651, victim of another shipwreck.

The most famous pirate to be executed at Execution Dock in Wapping was, of course, Captain Kidd, in 1701, but Kidd was not by any stretch a local man. Born in Scotland, he appears to have started his 'career' in America, his cut-throat crew being recruited from the New York area. Unfortunately for him, one of the ships he captured – the 500-ton *Quedagh Merchant*, was Indian owned, and resulted in a complaint to the East India Company, ending in a warrant being issued for his arrest. The aftermath was particularly unpleasant in that his body – which had broken the first noose, necessitating a second – was left hanging to rot as a warning to others.

HERE COME THE WITCHES

By the time James I took over the throne from Elizabeth, the number of executions for witchcraft had declined, and there was less support for his virtual campaign against witches. So he instigated the 1604 Witchcraft Act, which changed the law so that hanging became mandatory for a first offence, even if no one had died as a result.

Joan Peterson, 'The Witch of Wapping', lived on Spruce Island (near Shadwell) and was perhaps just attempting to help the sick, as did so many in the seventeenth century in areas affected by overcrowding and poverty, the resultant illnesses especially prevalent among non-mariners. Some thought there was more to it, and at her Old Bailey trial it was said that 'the Devil often came to suck her, sometimes in the likeness of a Dog, and at other times like a Squirrel' – such 'evidence' obviously provided by those she had failed to cure. Sadly for her, she also owned a black cat (!) and she was hanged at Tyburn in 1652.

Others were luckier. Joan Kent features in the Old Bailey trials of 1682. Because her case rested on an incident in Spitalfields, the assumption is that she would have lived nearby. The accusation of witchcraft stemmed from her desire to buy two pigs on credit from 'Mr Chambler', but credit was refused, the pigs then becoming sick, and his 5-year-old daughter developing swellings 'all over her body' resulting in her death. Another witness swore that Joan had a teat on her back (with which to feed a 'familiar') and another swore that she had overturned his coach when he refused to carry her. However, Joan convinced the jury that she was a good, honest, church-going woman and they found her not guilty.

Anna Trapnel, the daughter of a Poplar shipwright, served around four months in a variety of prisons in 1654 on being accused of witchcraft, with some it seemed regarding her as saint rather than sinner. Anti-Cromwell, she was a passionate preacher and had one of several spiritual revelations when at 'John Simpson's church in Aldgate' (possibly St Olave's nearer modern-day Fenchurch Street). It was in Cornwall that she was accused of witchcraft, leading to her trial, while back in London she was revered as a prophet. Certainly she had a way with words, and was adept at talking her way out of tight corners.

Living in Red Lion Street, Spitalfields, Nicholas Culpeper was a famous herbalist at the time, treating patients at his pharmacy in Commercial Street, Shoreditch, without charging the poor, to the fury of medical colleagues. He gave advice on health and wrote books about herbal cures. A widow from Shoreditch accused him of witchcraft in 1643 and he was imprisoned, but the story goes that the widow had not been cured of whatever ailed her and was taking her revenge with her accusation. It appears that although she was supported by the medical establishment, not happy with his 'free' cures, his trial resulted in acquittal.

MOMENTOUS MOVES

Both the East India Company (founded in 1600, becoming the largest international trader in London) and Trinity House (founded 1514 and responsible for providing buoys and lighthouses as well as supervising apprenticeships and operating a seamen's court) moved their main operation to the East End in the early part of the seventeenth century. The presence of the East India Company in Blackwall from 1614 made a big difference to employment in the Stepney area, and the company seems to have looked after its employees, building houses for them and providing for the women or widows whose husbands were injured or killed in their employ. They even founded a hospital at Poplar a decade later for maimed or aged sailors from the East India fleet.

In 1618, the working headquarters of Trinity House moved to Ratcliff, and then to Tower Hill after the Restoration (1660), this building destroyed in the Great Fire but duly replaced. Trinity House was also an outstanding employer – it was involved in charitable work, with almshouses for elderly seamen and their widows provided at several locations, and pensions provided to 160 people by 1618, increasing to 1,100 by 1681. Some of these almshouses remain in the Mile End Road, with the central building (allegedly designed by Sir Christopher Wren) distinguished by the model ships above the doors.

Entrance to almshouses in Mile End Road. *Author's collection*

Moving in a different direction were the three ships under the command of Captain John Smith that left Blackwall in 1606 carrying the first settlers to Virginia. Fourteen years later, sixty-five people joined the *Mayflower*, a ship partly owned by Robert Sheffield of Blackwall. Some of these passengers were from Aldgate, Whitechapel and Shoreditch, all seeking new lives and a new freedom from religious impositions.

THE EARLY 'PEN AND INK'

It wasn't just the stink of the plague pits that dominated the air of the East End during the time of the Stuarts. It was also the growth of some pretty smelly industries, located deliberately east of the city walls as they were banned inside. Sir William Petty, doctor and polymath who advised both Cromwell and James II, wrote in the seventeenth century of 'the fumes steams and stinks of the whole easterly pyle'.

There were lime kilns in Limehouse and slaughterhouses in Aldgate in the area that became known as Butcher's Row. Bow also became a centre for the slaughter of cattle for the city, with the stench of blood and offal that resulted (cattle bones were later put to contrasting use in the manufacture of what became famous porcelain). Around Whitechapel and Aldgate, the leather-tanning trade used animal dung and urine as part of the process, the latter also used in the local manufacture of alum (a dye). Similarly, horse manure was used in forming the outside of the bells manufactured at the Whitechapel Bell Foundry. In Goodman's Yard, Wellclose Square and Rosemary Lane (all in and around Aldgate) were glass factories by the seventeenth century, plus at least two more in Ratcliff which specialised in bottle glass, one of these (Nelson and Co.) run by a group of sea captains. Close by, in what is now Glasshouse Fields (of course), another factory specialised in window glass from 1691. On the

River Lea, at the very edge of the East End, one of the bigger mills had introduced the production of gunpowder, another toxic smell. Then there was the leper hospital in Mile End – and lepers begging in the area around St Dunstan's – adding to the noxious fumes of this period.

Joseph Truman joined the malodorous Black Eagle brewery in Brick Lane in 1666, supplying beer to the fire-fighters in the Great Fire of London. He took over the lease in 1679 and grew the business, which had its own granary and stables.

The influx of brothels in the seventeenth century tend to be included in any list of 'stink' industries, with Damaris Page probably its most famous madam, or, as Samuel Pepys described her, 'great bawd of the seamen'. Born in Stepney, she became a teenage prostitute, progressing over the next fifteen years to running two brothels. One

Truman's brewery. *Author's postcard collection*

was for ordinary seamen in Ratcliff Highway, the other in Rosemary Lane for the richer naval officers who could afford more expensive prostitutes. Women were recruited from local widows or those with husbands fighting overseas. Damaris, a victim of the Bawdy House Riots (see above), became famous for her petition in 1668 to the (also scandal-ous!) Countess of Castlemaine – The Poor Whores' Petition. This craved protection for their 'venereal pleasures'. The broth-els enabled Damaris to invest heavily in property and she died a wealthy woman in her Ratcliff Highway home in 1669, despite serving three years for manslaughter following her part in an illegal abortion – being pregnant seems to have saved her from hanging. Mass raids on brothels in Shoreditch, Wapping and Ratcliff (as well as Central London) during the reigns of James I and Charles I had little effect, and although prostitution was declared a public nuisance, rather than a crime, in 1641, the Puritanical rule of Cromwell which followed was a step backwards.

POPULATION GROWTH

After the Great Fire of London, there was a large increase in the population of the East End, with people moving away from the perceived risk. However, although in Shadwell alone there were 700 dwellings by 1650, most of these were still timber built. Some were now made of brick, bearing in mind that in 1605 there had been a royal proclamation necessitating that new builds should be of stone and brick to preserve as much timber as possible for shipping – a proclamation which proved futile, and not only in Shadwell. John Stow mentioned in his 1603 *Survay* [sic] that elm trees had been felled to make room for tenements here. This particular part of the East End had enough residents to necessitate it having its own water supply by the 1680s, using water from the Thames, and could boast fifty-five shops, a market and forty-four taverns or alehouses by 1681 – while no doubt still retaining a whipping post with whipping being a common punishment for all kinds of misdemeanours (as listed in the Old Bailey proceedings of the period).

St Dunstan's needed extra accommodation by the end of the seventeenth century to cope with the influx. The new residents were more likely to have been in manufacturing industries than, as previously, agricultural. Additionally, silk-weaving, especially among the Huguenots along the western borders of the East End, proliferated as the new-comers obtained exclusive rights to manufacture certain classes of silk goods. The import of European silk goods was banned, and from 1701 so were Oriental silks, leading a huge boost for the industry and adding to the number of weavers in and around Spitalfields.

While Gascoyne's 1703 map shows dense settlement near the city boundary and along the Thames, it also shows a large number of fields which were devoted to market gardening, so agriculture was still a feature of some parts of Mile End, Bethnal Green and Bow. This would have continued to be profitable because of the proximity of cus-tomers in London, whose population had grown to well over 674,000 by 1700.

The general influx was also due in part to the fact that Oliver Cromwell had officially allowed the Jews to return to England in 1656 – they had been expelled in 1290 by Edward I. Only a year later, they had established the first Jewish cemetery, off the Mile End Road, confirming their arrival and settlement in the East End. Aldgate was the site of the second synagogue to be built in the UK, in 1701. The first was close by, in the City of London, a few decades earlier. Cromwell's replacement of monarchy with 'Commonwealth' meant conflict with others with differing beliefs, such as the Quakers, who opened meeting houses in Mile End and what is now Quaker Street, Spitalfields, to provide places of wor-ship. Additionally, a large number of Scandinavians arrived in the seventeenth century, enough to merit their own church in Wellclose Square in 1696; many of these were in the timber trade, timber being a major import.

Other races were beginning to settle in the East End in the seventeenth century, with St Botolph's Aldgate parish register records particularly revealing. There are many references to the deaths of servants, e.g. on 8 September 1618, 'Burial of James an Indian servant to Mr James Duppa, beer brewer' and, interestingly, 'a blackmore wife' (i.e. not a servant) in April 1618 named as Anne Vause, married to 'Anthonie Vause, trumpeter', her husband possibly employed at the Tower of London nearby.

COME AND BUY

In *The History and Survey of London*, Volume II, by B. Lambert (written in 1806) there is a reference to a 1606 act saying that 'no foreigner whatsoever should presume to vend his, her or their goods in the City, by connivance or otherwise, either in shop, house, stall or street upon the penalty of £5 for every offence except such as brought provisions to the City'. This is why so many hawkers and traders ended up just over the city boundary in what was then called Hog Lane (later Rosemary Lane and later still Royal Mint Street). Although this area was initially occupied by rich merchants, they moved out following the twin disasters of plague and fire, and small houses grew apace in crowded streets round about.

It was probably Hog Lane that Alexander Pope refers to as a 'Rag Fair' in the following century (in his poem *The Dunciad*, 1728) – as being a place selling 'old cloathes and frippery'. This Rag Fair was also regarded as a useful way of offloading stolen goods.

It was not only trade around Hog Lane that flourished, because in 1664 Charles II initiated a 'weekly market at Ratcliff Cross and an annual fair on Michaelmas Day at Mile End Green or other convenient place' (*East London Observer*, 29 December 1866). Charles was obviously a fan of markets, because he also implemented a charter in 1682 giving permission for a market at Spital Field on Thursdays and Saturdays.

The fanatical Oliver Cromwell was not such a fan, of course, but the Green Goose Fair at Bow held every Whitsun seems to have avoided his radar. It was established by 1630, Green Goose also being a term for immoral women. The fair's drunken and rowdy crowds were described by poet John Taylor, but it survived until the nineteenth century, and even has a plaque in Fairfield Road mentioning its closure 'due to rowdyism and vice'.

VISITORS' VIEWS

In June 1671, Sir Christopher Wren had visited the Brick Lane area, a place he described as 'unpassable for Coach, adjoyning to Durty lands of meane habitations & farr from any Church'. As Surveyor General, he commented on a planning application in 1673 for housing at Mile End as being a place 'more wholesome' than its neighbours.

Samuel Pepys was a regular visitor to the East End, which was just a few miles from his base near the Tower. In 1661, for example, he visited Margetts' ropeyard in Limehouse and apparently decided to use them to supply the navy in his role as Naval Comptroller – Ropemakers' Fields, an area of parkland, marks the spot. He also recorded a trip to lime kilns at the jetty just along from the

Bunch of Grapes in Narrow Street (now the Grapes). The following April he stood outside a draper's at Aldgate to watch three men who had collaborated against Charles I on their way to the gallows at 'Tiburne' where they were hanged, drawn and quartered. Such sights seemed to be very much a popular entertainment at the time. He made several visits to the Rose and Crown in Mile End with his wife, favouring their salmon, or to the Queen's Head at Bow, which he described as a 'resort'. He also recorded a 1663 visit to his friend Sir William Rider in Bethnal Green 'by coach'. As part of his job, he took the occasional hackney carriage to Wapping or to Blackwall, to inspect the East India Company's warehouses.

THE THREE RS

Sir John Jolles seems to have acquired his wealth via his wife, but he was also a successful Bow draper who went on to be Lord Mayor of London. In 1613 he used some of his wealth to open the John Jolles School for Boys in Bow, a free school intended for thirty-five boys from 'Stratford Bow and St Leonard Bromley', soon acquiring the status of a grammar school. However, by 1711, it appeared to be teaching literally just the three Rs, and was helped along by a merger with Coborn School. This had been established in 1701 by philanthropist Prisca Coborn, a wealthy Bow brewer's wife, who, in her will, left money for a Bow charity school for local children 'of the poor inhabitants'. Boys were taught reading, writing and accounting, with girls, predictably, taught reading, writing and … needlework. The two schools operated as one from a picturesque gabled building next to Bow Church, the ground floor used as an open 'marketplace' with a 'cage for disciplining refractory boys' and a lock-up for 'vagrants', according to the *East London Observer* of 2 November 1912. The Coborn School later also united with the Coopers' Company School (see Chapter Five) and survives in Essex.

The artist and courtier Sir Balthazar Gerbier, who lived in a house in Bethnal Green inherited from his jeweller father-in-law, was less interested in philanthropy. In 1649, he opened an academy nearby for elite young men focusing on astronomy, navigation, engraving, architecture, military discipline and elocution. He also gave lectures, including to 'ladies and honourable women', on public speaking. The *Oxford Dictionary of National Biography* describes his academy as 'effectively a school for spies' since the curriculum also included foreign languages, cosmography and the construction of military fortifications. It only survived until 1660. The rector of St Mary Matfelon, Whitechapel, Ralph Davenant, founded the Davenant Foundation Grammar School in 1680 to provide free education to forty poor local boys and thirty girls. They were educated in the principles of religion as well as the basics, and the modern version survives in Essex. A wealthy silk merchant from Bethnal Green, Thomas Parmiter, left money for a school for ten poor children, plus almshouses for the elderly. The school was built in St John Street, off Brick Lane, in around 1682, later moving to what became Parmiter Street until being wiped out in a 1945 air raid.

The children of the East End had reason to give thanks to such philanthropists for their education, assuming it was appreciated, as it would be another two centuries before the Education Acts came into force. Those from more affluent families had more choice, including a boarding school in Bethnal Green from *c.* 1700, specialising in Latin, and headed up by classicist Robert Ainsworth, a man with enlightened anti-corporal punishment views.

GETTING TIDDLY

Legend has it that the Hoop and Grapes in Aldgate escaped the Great Fire of London in 1666 by just yards, but historians feel that the building is dated a few years later and that it probably started life as something other than a drinking establishment. The legend is far more interesting! It continues as a Grade II listed, timber-framed pub.

By the end of the seventeenth century there were forty-four taverns spread among the Ratcliff and Shadwell dwellings – everything from a simple taproom to larger establishments like the Queen's Head in Ratcliff Highway with its two bars and six drinking rooms. There were a lot of thirsty mariners to cater for, after all. This was, incidentally, a different Queen's Head to the one Pepys favoured in Bow.

Two pubs in Aldgate were established by 1681: the Blue Boar and the Three Nuns. This is when they are first recorded as being regular stopping-off points (and starting points) for coach services to and from Essex destinations such as Harwich, Chelmsford, Epping and Maldon (*The City Press*, 2 August 1863). These were daily services, run by private enterprise. The Blue Boar closed when the railway opened nearby and was demolished in the nineteenth century, and the Three Nuns met a similar fate a century later.

Gin drinking originated in Holland in the seventeenth century but did not take long to hit British shores. A few decades later, following the Restoration, it was being used as a medicinal remedy. Some of the mills in Bromley-by-

Three Nuns, Aldgate. *National Brewery Heritage Trust*

Bow were used to grind the grain needed for distillation, supplying the newly arrived gin palaces as well as the many taverns and the newly dubbed 'public houses'.

During excavations in 1999 an unopened bottle of dry Madeira from Portugal or Greece was discovered, dated to around 1679, in the wine cellar of the Master Gunner of England in Spitalfields. The British palate was obviously expanding its horizons, in the East End as elsewhere, with further expansion – of different kinds – following.

7

GEORGIANS

When Queen Anne died after losing seventeen children, a century of Georges followed (1714–1830), with a period of colonisation and the first Prime Minister. The East End, as in previous centuries, took it all in its stride, continuing to expand, to absorb the Agricultural Revolution and the start of the Industrial Revolution, and to involve its large maritime population along the Thames in the battles with France. Even the famous mutiny on the *Bounty* in 1789 could be said to have started in Wapping, because Captain Bligh was living there when he set sail with Fletcher Christian – and supposedly inspected the *Bounty* prior to their voyage.

NOT JUST NAVAL BATTLES

The introduction of a new machine in March 1767 for 'the more expeditious and exact sawing of timber' near Limehouse 'to be worked by the wind' was not welcomed by local sawyers. 'A large body of sawyers assembled and pulled down the saw mills latterly erected … on pretence that it deprived many workmen of employment' less than two months later. The following January, John Smith was sentenced 'to suffer seven years imprisonment at Newgate, to pay a fine, and to enter into recognizance for his good behaviour' when he was found guilty of 'riotous assembly' and destroying another local saw mill (*East London Observer*, 18 January 1913).

The Spitalfields Riots by local weavers and throwsters (silk winders) were caused by a number of factors during the 1760s: cheap silk smuggled in from France, poor rates of pay and engine looms putting hand-loom weavers out of work. Secret societies (the forerunner of trade unions) attacked and destroyed a number of silk works in the area, until soldiers raided a Spitalfields pub meeting and arrested the ringleaders, two of whom were hanged near the Salmon and Ball pub in Bethnal Green (1769). Similarly, Spitalfields weavers in 1768 'forcibly entered the house of Nathaniel Farr in Pratt's-alley and cut to pieces and destroyed the silk-work manufactory, and murdered a lad of seventeen, one Edward Fitchett' (*East London Observer*, 18 January 1913).

In the 1700s it was actually illegal to wear chintz in England because of legislation designed to protect the silk weavers, who were unable to produce it, in addition to protecting the production of English linen and wool. The same article in the *East London Observer* mentions ladies 'convicted before the Lord Mayor' for wearing 'chintz gowns'. In fact, weavers were rioting as early as 1719 when imported cheap calico became fashionable, attacking women wearing it with ink or even ripping off the offending garment. It wasn't until 1801, when various acts had regularised prices and wages, that these riots finally came to an end: by the 1830s the industry had declined to the status of 'sweat shop' production.

In 1768, the coal heavers and watermen working around Wapping had had enough of unpaid wages and assembled 'riotously' week after week in 'Stepney Fields' and elsewhere as far as the City of London. Again, the *East London Observer* (18 January 1913) gives historic accounts of many assemblies which dissolved into riots 'attended with much bloodshed' with 'flags flying, drums beating', the situation aggravated by sailors 'long detained in the River by the coal heavers refusing to work' who had 'begun to deliver their ship themselves' resulting in 'a body of coal heavers' attacking the sailors with 'many lives' lost. By June 1768 they were 'grown a terror to the whole neighbourhood of Stepney and Wapping, and commit the most shocking outrages' to such an extent that 'the military was called in to the assistance of the civil power' with 'twenty of the desperadoes apprehended'. Although two coal heavers were executed for murder at Tyburn on 11 July the rioting continued, as did the executions, with another seven being executed on 26 July at Sun Tavern Fields 'near Stepney' after rioting in protest at low wages, with '50,000 being present at the execution'. Local executions were used as a deterrent to local rioters, although not always effective. A further twenty were transported after what seemed to be very brief trials at the Old Bailey. The last public execution – and entertainment – at the Tower, incidentally, was that of Lord Lovat in April 1767, when a dozen people died following the collapse of a spectators' stand.

Riots seemed to increase rather than diminish as the months wore on. 'Five or six hundred' sailors 'riotously assembled at Limehouse' in August 1768 (the same newspaper gives the account) boarding several outward-bound ships, preventing their sailing 'until the seamen's wages were increased' – although these were dispersed by the local guard, at a time pre-dating the establishment of a fully formed police force in the area. The newspaper commends the 'vigilance of Sir John Fielding's officers' who were able to disperse such 'riotous assemblies' without much bloodshed. The anti-Catholic Gordon riots of 1780 resulted in the chapel in Virginia Street, Shadwell, being destroyed in spite of strong defence from the Irish and the military.

The Irish were not the only locals breaking the law. In 1813, 500 Chinese from two opposing clans (the Chenies and the Chin Choo) became involved in gang violence over a small, disputed debt of just 1s 6d. Their knife-wielding battle took place in the East India Company's barracks at Shadwell, with three people killed – one with his 'bowels ripped open' according to *The Times* of 30 September 1813 – and seventeen wounded, including the memorably named Too Sugar of the Chin Choos.

By 1826, there were still problems with 'lawless gangs' of up to 600 attacking individuals and businesses in and around Spitalfields, resulting in a deputation from the 'parish of Bethnal Green' requesting help from Mr Peel, the Home Secretary (*Morning Advertiser*, 19 September 1826). Peel gave orders for forty mounted men to patrol the area night and day, based at Cambridge Heath Gate, Mile End Gate, Whitechapel Church and near the Regent's Canal in the Mile End Road. Their formidable presence did indeed seem to make a difference.

A VARIETY OF CRIMES AND PUNISHMENTS

Debtors

There were so many taxes and rates to be paid in London in the eighteenth century that it was not overly surprising to find that Whitechapel had its own debtors' prison. Rates were payable for the Church, the poor, the watch (pre-police), lighting (lamp rate), street cleansing (scavenger rate), land tax, etc. In May 1776, the prison held twenty-three debtors, but this had increased by 1783 because the *East London Observer* of 29 May 1915 gives an account of more than forty prisoners escaping from 'Whitechapel Jail' that year by 'making a breach through the wall of the jail-yard into an adjacent garden'. There was also a small prison in nearby Wellclose Square underneath a pub called the Cock and Neptune, with the landlord also acting as gaoler. This landlord would benefit commercially as the person whom debtors had to pay for food and drink, which was not provided. A reconstruct of one of the cells here was displayed at the Museum of London in the summer of 2019.

Theft

You could be sentenced to death for stealing linen, like Thomas Gowen and Joseph Pewterer of Shadwell in 1715, or for stealing a watch worth 6s like John Cook, the robbery taking place 'between Stepney and Whitechapel' in 1773 (*Leeds Intelligencer*, 22 June). If you were lucky, you could escape with a whipping, like John Hague in 1783 who stole a ham in Whitechapel. Or you could be transported to the other side of the world for, say, seven years, like Ellen Morgan from Shadwell who was reported for charging for false predictions of the future in 1834. If you were a 'respectable' magistrate and churchwarden, like Joseph Merceron from Bethnal Green, you might get just eighteen months in prison for embezzling money from the Poor Fund for personal use (1818).

Animal 'Sport'

While thieves, con artists and embezzlers continue to appear in our courts, at least bull-baiting, cock-fighting, bear-baiting and pugilism have disappeared, being described as appealing to 'the lower orders' rather than 'indoor amusements' in the eighteenth century, according to the *History of the London Stage*. Interestingly, the author James Boswell, in his journals of 1762–3, mentions Wapping as one of the places where cock-fighting was practised, and felt that the 'sport' was attracting 'young aristocrats'. The 1835 Cruelty to Animals Act put an end to such sport, although no mention was made of rats, leaving a loophole available to some East End publicans.

On the Thames

Crime on the river was particularly rife in the eighteenth century, with smuggling and theft at the forefront. The cargo ships moored at Ratcliff were easy targets. Any man not in the navy was also an easy target – they fell victim to the press gangs operating out of local pubs such as the Bell at Wapping and the Black Boy and Trumpet at St Katherine's stairs. Men were, of course, desperately needed between 1756 and 1763 during the Seven Years War, which started as a conflict between the French and English over territory but escalated into a global affair, necessitating tens of thousands more seamen. Apart from the press gangers, men could also be kidnapped by crimpers for the army or the merchant (not Royal) navy, and then sold on to the highest bidder.

Cattle as Weapons

Some crimes made good use of the cattle being driven through the East End to Smithfield Market. One crowd used a bullock as a battering ram to smash their way into a

Spitalfields warehouse, while another regular gang fright-
ened cattle into charging down passers-by, who would be
robbed while on the ground.

Prostitution

While coffee houses springing up in the City of London
at this time were probably just that in the main, the bagn-
ios (which provided coffee and Turkish baths!) offered a
little more, especially in the East End, with one particularly well-known bagnio in Alie Street: the Turk's Head, a
known brothel. There is an account in the *Derby Mercury*
of 23 February 1753 regarding a court case one week
earlier. Mary Cunningham was tried at Hicks's Hall, just
north of Smithfield, along with three others, for 'keeping
disorderly houses in the Parish of St Mary, Whitechapel'.
All were found guilty, and Mary was sentenced to:

> Stand in or upon the Pillory in Ayliff-Street, once within
> there three Months, for two hours, to pay a Fine of One
> Shilling, and to be imprisoned in His Majesty's Gaol of
> Newgate for twelve Months. Two are to stand in the pillory
> the corner of Ayliff-street, Goodman's Fields on Monday
> next, and to suffer six Months Imprisonment in Newgate;
> the other is to lie in Bridewell for one month.

Hicks Hall was the centre for Middlesex 'sessions' when
the county of Middlesex included all of London north of
the Thames, excepting the City of London. Bridewell was
the city's first house of correction, closing in 1855. There
is also a fascinating account in *The Weekly Journal* of
5 October 1728 of a constable and his assistants appre-
hending 'nine male ladies' during a raid on 'Miss' Jonathan

Muff's molly house (a place to indulge in what was illegal homosexuality) in Black Lion Yard, Whitechapel. They were charged with 'the detestable Sin of Sodomy' and punished by being whipped or fined.

Later the same century, pubs along the Ratcliff Highway were also devoted to prostitution – the White Swan, the Gunboat, the Malt Shovel, the Globe and Artichoke. As for streetwalkers, these haunted the same areas as the criminal underworld, i.e. Rosemary Lane in East Smithfield, Whitechapel and Shadwell. A report by the London Guardian Society for Preventing Prostitution in 1817 gave some statistics that were perhaps not too surprising – a figure of 1,000 prostitutes working in Shadwell alone, an area with just over 1,000 houses at the time, and sixty-five brothels in and around Commercial Road, Stepney.

Pirates

Execution Dock in Wapping was still in service thanks to pirating being an ongoing problem. These executions were reported nationally, e.g. 'Four pirates executed at Execution Dock' and 'all to be hung in chains' (*Newcastle Courant*, 12 March 1737). The 31-year-old 'Captain William Lawrence, Commander of the *Pluto* Privateer, was convicted' for 'piracy and robbery committed on the High Seas' having robbed the Dutch ship *Enighadt* of three 'bales of cambric value £700, two bales of bed ticking value £100 and other goods'. He was carried in a cart from Newgate to Execution Dock (*Derby Mercury*, 7 December 1759 and *Oxford Journal*, 22 December 1759).

Two of the four pirates who 'ran away' with the *King George* privateer of Bristol – and cut off the nose of its captain – were convicted of mutiny under the names

Captain Smith alias Thomas Harding and his assistant Robert Main or Mayne. Both were executed at Execution Dock. Newspaper reports went on to say that the corpse of one 'was carried to a relation in Whitechapel' who refused to bury him, passing him to another 'relation in Spitalfields' who also refused 'that friendly office'! This apparently resulted in the body being sold, 2*d* being offered to each person who took away the body to be buried 'decently', although the number of persons is not given (*Ipswich Journal*, 1 May 1762 and *Bath Chronicle*, 20 May 1762).

And the Rest!

While there is not space to detail the long list of assaults, attacks by highwaymen, and the various murders during the Georgian period in the East End (enough for more than one book!), mention has to be made of the infamous Ratcliff Highway Murders, the seven victims presumed murdered by John Williams, who was found guilty, committing suicide in prison in December 1811. Similarly famous, Bethnal Green had its own version of Burke and Hare, i.e. its own Resurrectionists, in the form of Williams (not the same one), Bishop, Fields and May. They lived in the unpleasant surroundings of Nova Scotia Gardens on the Shoreditch border in 1831, an area once used for brick-making that had left behind damp, unpleasant hovels. They were found guilty of murdering innocent victims to fill the shortage of cadavers required by the main London hospitals – fewer people were being executed than in the previous century, providing fewer bodies for dissection. Bishop and Williams were hanged, the others cleared as accessories. Gibbets were used to hang the bodies of criminals in very public

Dick Turpin.
Motif collection

places such as by the Mile End Milestone, the Bow Milestone and in Whitechapel Road as a deterrent, until the practice was abolished in 1834. And, even more famous, Dick Turpin is said to have shot and killed his partner-in-crime Tom King in 1738 in a scuffle outside the Red Lion in Aldgate where they had stabled a stolen horse called White Stockings – Turpin seems to have shot King by mistake because he thought he was a constable.

SOMETHING EQUALLY NASTY

Slave ships arrived regularly on the shore at Wapping in the eighteenth century, usually docking at the Town of Ramsgate inn. Local man John Newton made at least three trips between 1750 and 1754 as part of the trade, with the

Town of
Ramsgate.
*Lesley Love, via
Facebook*

Gentleman's Magazine of 1764 estimating that 20,000 black slaves were established in London. It seems that the Black Boy and Trumpet at St Katherine's Stairs was a particularly popular, and convenient, venue for such buying and selling, its name perhaps a reminder that 'musical' slaves were particularly popular. Although many were brought simply to be sold, others were 'brought hither as personal servitors by Naval and Mercantile officers on return from their lengthened cruises'. Some of these unfortunates managed to escape, and a William Webb of 'Limehouse Hole' in

1720 advertised a reward of half a guinea 'and reasonable charges' in the 4 August issue of *The Daily Post* for the return of a 'negro man, about 20 years old, called Dick … [with] wool hair' and the word 'Hare' tattooed on his chest. Apparently it was not an unusual sight to see black children begging in the East End streets, presumably more escapees. The luckier ones could end up in grand uniforms working for rich merchants in Stepney.

NOT MORE DEPRAVITY?

In Shakespeare's time, theatres had an unsavoury reputation as centres of immorality. Even more than 100 years later, when the Goodman's Fields Theatre opened in 1727, it was not welcomed by the 'grave and respectable citizens who dreaded that their daughters and servants might be contaminated by the close vicinity' and, indeed, the location was surrounded, apparently, by 'a halo of brothels' (*East London Observer*, 16 September 1911). It promptly closed, then reopened in another building nearby in 1732, finally attaining some respectability when the most famous actor of the period, David Garrick, appeared there in 1741, debuting in *Richard III*. He was so well known and popular that the roads around Goodman's Fields were 'nightly blocked up by the carriages of the nobility and gentry'. The *East London Observer* pointed out that although the theatre was 'in truth, a dingy den in a very dubious neighbourhood' the 'world of fashion was trooping down the Whitechapel Road to see the new wonder'. However this, too, lasted only another year or so, with yet another venue replacing it and lasting until sometime early in the nineteenth century.

The New Wells had a similar struggle, opening in 1737 in Mill Yard (off Cable Street) but threatened with closure as a disorderly house two years later. In 1744, it was one of four theatres presented before the 'Grand Jury of Middlesex' as 'places kept apart for the encouragement of luxury, extravagance, idleness and other wicked illegal purposes' but limped along until 1752, specialising apparently in balancing acts e.g. rope dancing (*Gentleman's Magazine*, 1813). Then there was the Royalty, which opened in Wellclose Square in 1787 and managed to hang on to its audiences until being destroyed by fire in 1826. It was replaced in 1828 by the Royal Brunswick Theatre, which lasted just three days before collapsing, killing at least ten people. Theatre did not seem to be the East End's forte, or, at least, not yet.

SALVATION IS NIGH

Three churches designed and built by Nicholas Hawksmoor arrived to cater for the growing population: Christ Church in Spitalfields and St Anne's in Limehouse in 1729 and St George's-in-the-East, Wapping, in 1730. The parish church of Bethnal Green, St Matthew's, opened its doors to its 15,000 residents in 1746 (with a watch house added on eight years later to keep out the body-snatchers). To cater for the growing ethnicity of the area, the first Swedish church in London opened in Prince's Square, Wapping, now Swedenborg Gardens, in 1729. This was the Ulrika Eleanora church, demolished *c*. 1921. (Jenni Lind, the 'Swedish nightingale' is said to have attended services here.) The first Danish church in London was also in this location (Prince's Square), seemingly pre-dating the

Swedish church by a dozen years but closed between 1840 and 1850. Brick Lane saw the arrival of Le Neuve Eglise, a Huguenot church, in 1743, the largest of the eleven French churches opened east of the city walls since 1687. And not forgetting the Germans (many of whom were specialist sugar-bakers), because in 1762 St George's German Lutheran Church was founded in what is now Alie Street, Whitechapel.

John Wesley made frequent visits to the East End between 1738 and 1790, his last just months before his death. He records accounts of preaching at local churches such as St George's-in-the-East at Wapping and St Paul's at Shadwell in addition to 'field preaching' in such locations as Ratcliffe Square. He consecrated a new Methodist preaching house in Poplar in 1772. His journal of 15 January 1777 refers to a visit to the parishioners of St Matthew's (Bethnal Green) where he saw a scene which caused him more 'distress' than in 'the prison of Newgate' thanks to the sight of 'one poor man ... creeping out of his sickbed to his ragged wife and three little children, who were more than half naked and the very picture of famine. When one brought in a loaf of bread, they all ran, seized upon it, and tore it in pieces in an instant.'

In 1758, Dr William Todd founded the Magdalen Hospital near Goodman Fields for 'fallen women', where they worked long hours sewing and learning domestic duties with the little spare time left taken up with religious instruction. Over 2,000 women were 'saved' in this way, with other homes following.

The Justice of the Peace (and novelist) Henry Fielding was responsible for forming a paid police force, the Bow Street Runners, active from 1770 in Shoreditch, Shadwell and Whitechapel (plus other London areas). Whitechapel was better policed than other areas as it seems to have been at the centre of East London crime at this period, with even Dick Turpin described (in the *East London Advertiser* of 23 August 1902) as a 'constant guest' at the White House and at Tyler's Ferry 'near Joe Sowter's cock-pit at Temple Mills' in the 1730s, somewhere 'few police officers were bold enough to approach'. Turpin's gang, the Gregories, were known to have been Wapping men.

The River Police were established in Wapping in 1798 complete with cutlasses and blunderbusses; they were taken over by the newly established Metropolitan Police of Robert Peel in 1839. This certainly helped reduce the scale of plundering the vessels suffered, although the high walls built round the West India and London Dock were also contributory.

TALKING OF DOCKS ...

Maritime commerce and shipbuilding continued to expand during the Georgian era. The first Thames-built steamship, *City of Edinburgh*, was launched in 1821 at Blackwall at a time when the industry was flourishing and new shipyards were opening in and around the area. William Fairbairn's shipyard in Millwall, for example, built 120 iron ships in its first decade or so after opening in 1835.

Here's a timeline of how the docks grew and changed the face of the East End in less than half a century:

1789: Brunswick Dock opened (Blackwall) with its tall mast house for fitting masts, its cranes for lifting guns and heavy store, and nearby coppers for boiling the blubber from the Greenland arrivals.

1802: West India Dock opened (Isle of Dogs) for imports, four years later for exports.

1805: London Dock opened (Wapping) with the loss of twenty-four mean streets and 120 ramshackle houses – it specialised in rice, tobacco, wine, wool and brandy.

1806: East India Dock opened (Blackwall) incorporating Brunswick (which was rebuilt for export).

1812: Tobacco Dock opened, its warehouses covering more than 5 acres.

1828: St Katharine Docks opened, with 1,250 houses – and the Royal Foundation of St Katharine – pulled down to make way for it.

A NEED FOR A HOSPITAL OR TWO ...

In spite of the demolition of housing to make way for the docks developments, and a number of destructive fires, the population of Tower Hamlets continued to grow – from *c*. 144,000 in 1801 (the time of the UK's first census) to *c*. 262,000 in 1831. This meant that there was an essential requirement for a hospital for the residents, many of whom still lived in appalling conditions with a high mortality rate. Up until the middle of the eighteenth century, the population had relied on local midwives, barber-surgeons, physicians (and quacks) who charged fees. The London Hospital was finally built in still semi-rural Whitechapel, opening fully in 1759 and replacing the London Infirmary in Prescot Street, the latter becoming

To the COMMITTEE of the Corporation of ⟶ LONDON-HOSPITAL.

The original London Hospital. *Wellcome Images*

a home for prostitutes, in an area which sported many such. One particular operation there hit the headlines fifteen years later when a carpenter (a Mr Scott) had his arm amputated after being shot by burglars (*East London Observer*, 28 August 1915). The Whitechapel site featured purpose-built operating theatres from the date it opened, although operations – including amputations – had been carried out earlier without making the headlines, according to the Royal London Hospital Archives.

A Jews' Hospital had already opened in Leman Street in 1747. Incidentally, Captain James Cook, explorer and navigator, who moved from Shadwell to Assembly Row, Mile End in 1765, contributed to the health of the local seamen by discovering a treatment for scurvy: principally malt and sauerkraut!

The Shadwell Spa had a short career, with its waters said to provide a cure for 'all cutaneous distempers, as leprosy, and all breaking out of the body' as per the *Daily Advertiser* of 18 September 1742. The Spa's waters were even said to have cured one old horse of blindness (*East*

London Observer, 15 June 1912) but were described (*East London Observer*, 21 October 1911) as 'impregnated with sulphur, vitriol, steel and antimony' ... assuredly 'horribly nasty'. In addition, the difficulty of access, and competition from elsewhere, were no doubt among the reasons it failed – although it went on to flourish for different reasons when it was discovered to be ideal for 'fixing the colours of calico printers'.

Better news was the opening of a free dispensary in 1782 in Leman Street, Whitechapel, but this was restricted to providing medicine and advice, with a few other dispensaries dotted around. By that time, 120 inpatients were being catered for at the London Hospital, mainly from the manufacturing and maritime industries. By 1807, according to the *East London Observer* (28 August 1915) 220 inpatients were being treated, with 2,600 outpatients recorded for the previous year. It really came into its own during the first of several cholera outbreaks in 1832, when around 800 East Londoners died. Cholera wards were created in crowded workhouses at Whitechapel, Bethnal Green, Limehouse, Shadwell and Wapping. Even HMS *Dover* was called into service – as a hospital ship for 200 seamen moored initially off Limehouse, operating in spite of protests from the crew. Additionally, an Infirmary for Asthma, Consumption and Other Diseases of the Lungs was opened in Brushfield Street, Spitalfields, in 1814.

For the 'feeble-minded' there was the Bethnal Green 'madhouse' from 1726, in a building which started life as Kirby's Castle. Conditions here in 1815 were so scandalous that a parliamentary committee was convened, but it took a long time for the hundreds of neglected inmates (mainly paupers) to be released from their confinement in filthy, overcrowded conditions, chained up for hours on end. Fortunately, by the mid-nineteenth century, when it had nearly 1,000 'patients', it became one of the largest and best-run in the country, a 'model of mental healthcare' according to the Commissioners of Lunacy. There was apparently a similar asylum in Whitechapel, although this is less well documented.

BOOM TIME FOR INDUSTRY

The opening of London Hospital actually boosted some local industries because the institution needed coal, linen, kitchen equipment, food and drink in ever increasing quantities on a regular basis.

By 1820, 20 per cent of London's manufacturing industries were in the East End. Brewing was particularly big business. The largest breweries in the area were the already long-established Red Lion at St Katharine Dock, which expanded in the 1720s when the demand for porter, the 'working man's beer', increased, and Truman's in Spitalfields, which had started at the end of the seventeenth century as the Black Eagle brewery, becoming the biggest brewery in the world (the *world*) by 1873. So popular was Truman's beer that the Prince of Wales became a customer, and Ben Truman became Sir Benjamin in 1760. It closed in 1989 following a flurry of mergers, but the name remained, and it was actually reborn in 2013 in neighbouring Hackney. The Red Lion, later Hoare & Co., survived the area's redevelopment but was taken over by Charrington's in the 1930s, a brewery that originated in the mid-eighteenth century in Mile End, lasting until 1975.

Whitechapel's most famous brewery was the Albion, which started life in 1808 as a brewing business attached to the seventeenth-century Blind Beggar pub in Whitechapel, expanding eventually into Mann, Crossman and Paulin and even later to Watney Mann. (The Albion itself closed 1979.) Whitbread's, the first mass-production brewery, started life in Brick Lane in 1742, moving to the City of London a few decades later and continuing to expand until selling out in 2000 to Interbrew. However, this area was also overwhelmed with sugar refineries, soap-boilers, silk-works and all its allied trades. Cable Street specialised in rope-making, Ratcliff in glass-making and sugar-refining, the Curtain Road area of Shoreditch in furniture-making, Wapping in soap-making, Bow in china, with Bethnal Green expanding into boot- and shoe-making once the sewing machine came into use at the end of the Georgian period. The Ratcliff Gas Light and Coke Company was established in 1817.

The Limehouse pottery started out in 1745, with the innovative and more successful Bow porcelain factory on its heels, the River Lea providing a less bumpy journey for conveying such delicate produce than the roads, and the surrounding marshes a useful dumping ground for failures. There was a thriving export trade and a popular line in figurines of famous people as well as the ubiquitous kitchenware, with the Duke of Argyll regularly supplied by Bow.

A DIFFERENT LIFE FOR SOME

Almshouses had already opened in the East End, but by 1773 there were more than twenty, catering for pensioners and widows, funded by city companies (for their ex-employees) including the East India Company, of course.

Mile End
workhouse.
*Rob Higgins,
via Flickr*

Workhouses were less pleasant places, springing up from 1723 in the area, at least thirteen opening over the next six decades, with apparently another half-dozen so-called pauper farms run by private individuals to cope with the overflow. Official reports on local workhouses were not encouraging: Bethnal Green workhouse in Hare Street (now Cheshire Street) was said to be flogging boys, shaving their heads and putting them to work turning a huge iron wheel (1822) and eventually became just as crowded as the Mile End Workhouse, which had as many as five to a bed due to its crowded conditions in 1826. A few charitable trusts kept some out of the workhouse by paying out-relief, no more than 1s per week.

Philanthropists were often the lifeblood of the poor, in an area where the contrast between the rich in the large houses in pretty squares and the poverty-stricken in their unfit-for-purpose hovels in the next street could not be more marked. These were people like Andrew Reed from Shadwell, who took pity 'on some poor motherless children in Wapping' in 1811 and decided there was a need for 'an Institution for Orphan Children'. After holding meetings and fundraising at the King's Arms in Wellclose

Square, he purchased a property in Cannon Street Road, taking in two orphan girls under the charge of a matron in April 1814, expanding rapidly, becoming known as the London Orphan Asylum. Further houses were utilised, in Bethnal Green and in Hackney (the latter for boys) and the project was able to eventually purchase 8 acres and a large house in Clapton, a few miles north, for 3,500 guineas (*East London Observer*, 15 February 1913).

In 1797 Peter Bedford, a silk-weaving proprietor from Spitalfields, opened the Spitalfields Soup Society, serving 1,000 people each day. He was also instrumental in starting a working men's club (in Spicer Street) with a school nearby and a night shelter in Hoxton. An obituary in the *Gentleman's Magazine* of May 1783 refers to another wealthy silk merchant from Spitalfields, John Baker, who had taken on the guardianship of several orphan children, 'improving their fortunes' with 'a virtuous education which laid the foundation of their prosperity' thanks to 'his unremitting attention to their welfare'. Better known is Jeremy Bentham from Spitalfields, who contributed to the 1834 Poor Laws as well as later social and prison reforms.

When John Strype (a Spitalfields man) updated Stow's *Survay* [*sic*] in 1720, he referred to the annual Cockney Feast in Stepney which raised money for the main purpose of apprenticing poor children 'to the sea service'. The institution was patronised by several distinguished characters including the Duke of Montagu, and continued until late into the eighteenth century.

One 'profession' that attracted a number of East Enders, particularly those from the Jewish community, was that of boxing, an attractive proposition for the otherwise unskilled and poverty-stricken, which grew in popularity in the eighteenth century. The inventor of the uppercut, 'Dutch Sam'

Elias (1775–1816), came from Whitechapel and established a formidable reputation as a bare-knuckle fighter.
Daniel Mendoza (1764–1836) from Aldgate established an
academy in the city where boys could train, and they could
have no finer teacher than someone who was champion of
England, the East End's earliest folk hero, and someone who
had actually met George III. There is a blue plaque at his
one-time home in Paradise Row, Bethnal Green.

But other opportunities were also blossoming ...

THE THREE RS

Although charity schools were gradually being replaced by
National and British Schools, these were very basic – some
in just a large hall with one master and older pupils (called
monitors) instructing the younger ones. This was a cheap
option and one that continued until after Victoria was on
the throne. Nevertheless, charity schools lingered on, with
the one at Mile End opening in 1724.

Additionally, Wapping man Henry Raine founded his
first school (for fifty boys) in Old Gravel Lane in 1716,
taking in fifty girls two years later, and setting up a boarding school (for forty girls, to train as domestics) in 1736.
He even offered a dowry in a twice-yearly draw, providing two lucky girls with £100, a great deal of money in the
eighteenth century. His schools moved to various local sites
over the years, the 1719 building remaining in Wapping
(its main site in June 2019 was in Approach Road, Bethnal
Green but threatened with closure at this point). In 1778
John Noorthouck, the writer and indexer, listed twenty-
four free and charity schools in the East End, and there was
some basic education provided in the workhouses, so most

Left: The plaque commemorating boxer Daniel Mendoza in Paradise Row, Bethnal Green. *Simon Harriyott, via Flickr*

Below: The original Raines School. *Building News, 19 June 1885*

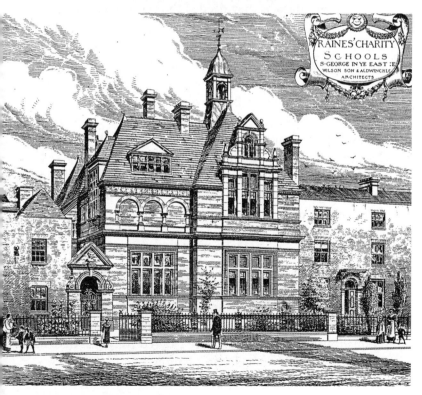

East End children had some sort of education available to them. Those boys interested in a career with the East India Company could attend a specialised academy in Bromley-by-Bow.

The wealthy residents from upmarket areas like Stepney Green could afford private tutors, but the wealthy were also instrumental in developing schooling in the East End. Spitalfields businessman Francis Bancroft left enough money in his will to establish almshouses (for twenty-four men) and a school for 100 poor boys. The school opened on the site of what is now Queen Mary's College in Bancroft Road, Mile End, in 1738, but moved out to Essex in Victorian times as they needed the extra space.

Back in Wapping, two Catholic schools (mainly catering for Irish immigrants) opened at this time – one attached to the Virginia Street chapel (1778) and one in Spicer Street, Spitalfields, in 1827. Another philanthropist, George Green, a Blackwall shipowner, funded not just one, but five, schools in Poplar from 1815 onwards (as well as a home for sailors and a row of almshouses). Not to be outdone, the Jews' Free School opened in 1817 in Spitalfields, supported by the Rothschilds, aiming to turn Jewish boys into English gentlemen. In spite of being sited next to a chicken slaughterhouse, it went on to become the largest of its kind, not just in the UK but in Europe. One Church of England school, which opened in 1710 for 110 local children, included tuition in the making and braiding of fishing nets: this was the Ratcliffe Hamlet School in Whitehorse Road, and survives with a new name (Stepney Greencoat) and location (Limehouse). All religions were catered for, with dissenters opening their own charity schools.

The East End poor no longer had any excuse for ignorance.

Jews' Free School hall, 1883. *The Builder, 7 July 1883*

A QUICK BUTCHER'S AT THE SURROUNDINGS

There were still farms with pigs and dairy herds in Bethnal Green, Mile End and Bow in the eighteenth century, and hay was the main crop from the pastures around Whitechapel (hence its regular haymarket). Oxen were reared on the rich grass of the Isle of Dogs, and the many windmills in Millwall and Whitechapel continued to produce flour. Whitechapel was becoming much more built up than its neighbours, Bethnal Green and Mile End, which still had large market gardens, but Whitechapel itself housed rich merchants and sea captains living cheek by jowl with working families in small houses or tenements. You can still find beautiful Georgian houses in Limehouse, Spitalfields and Stepney, but the tenements and small houses have long gone.

The Ratcliff area in particular was decimated by the loss of over 450 dwellings, twenty public buildings and thirty-six warehouses following a fire in 1794 that had started at a barge-builders, regarded as the biggest fire in the London area since 1666. Fires were a regular problem, but this one was on a different scale, changing the landscape, destroying smaller wharves and local businesses such as timber yards and rope-makers, 'cooperages and sugar houses' (*East London Observer*, 11 April 1914, quoting *Notes of Waterside History*).

This was a time of good and bad news. Locally, lasting traditions were beginning, such as the taste for eel pies – at least one tea room, called Clay Hall, in Blondin Street, Bow, had Londoners flocking to its doors during the eighteenth century to try this particular 'delicacy'. However, a reminder of the area's diversity is that such visitors also had to be careful on their way to Bow because of the large numbers of footpads and highwaymen along the Mile End Road.

8

VICTORIANS

A settled monarchy did not mean that the East End settled into some kind of cosy harmony. Far from it. There were too many battles to fight. They had even had to fight for a park: a petition to Queen Victoria with 30,000 signatories in 1840 resulted in the first public park to be built in London specifically for the people. The petition addressed an official 1839 report (from the Registrar General of Births, Deaths and Marriages) that a park would diminish the local annual death toll and add years to the lives of the East End population who lived with its overcrowding and polluted air.

THE STRUGGLE FOR SURVIVAL

With the import of French silk came the decline of the silk trade, and the once grand houses in Spitalfields and Shoreditch (in particular) were turned into multi-occupancy tenements. These were owned by middle-class landlords with no interest in their tenants or in improving conditions. The shipbuilding industry around the docks was also suffering from around 1866, with 27,000 of its workers unemployed at that stage. Many workers began migrating to the East End sweatshops, which produced clothing, shoes and furniture. Areas like the Old Nichol, off Shoreditch High Street,

'Free Dinners to Poor Children at the King Edward's Mission, Whitechapel – "Before." The Rush for the Door'. *The Graphic, 15 March 1890*

became famous for all the wrong reasons with Charles Booth's poverty maps at the end of the nineteenth century showing it as one of the 'blackest' (i.e. poorest) places to live, full of damp cramped dwellings, fetid passageways and non-existent sanitation. Similarly, articles such as that in the *Illustrated London News* of 15 February 1868, pointed out that areas like Bethnal Green were 'on the verge of pauperism'.

This was not an overnight failing, for Dr Hector Gavin, the Crimea's sanitary inspector, had written *Sanitary Ramblings* half a century earlier (1848) describing the ironically named Paradise Row in Bethnal Green as being awash with decomposing 'refuse' from cows and pigs, and Globe Road in Stepney similarly piled high with 'every variety of manure'. He also refers to Pleasant Place in Bethnal Green (these streets obviously not named by residents!) as 'filthy and abominable', being virtually a 'canal with a black, slimy compost of clay and putrescent animal remains'. Flower and Dean Street in Whitechapel was another notorious area with as many as sixty brothels, the area linked to all the Ripper victims. Poplar-born Arthur Morrison also wrote descriptions of the East End as, for example, 'an evil plexus of slums' where 'filthy men and women live on gin' (*Tales of Mean Streets*, 1894).

High mortality rates in the East End were reported regularly in the *Illustrated London News*, often attributed to recurrent bouts of cholera (1832, 1848–9, 1853–4, 1866). The Poor Law Act of 1834, which meant that able-bodied men had only the workhouse as a safety net, with no parish relief (local funding) available, only made things worse. The coroners' court records for the East End after this date give frequent accounts of death by starvation, often a result of a refusal to enter the workhouse. One particular account from the coroners' inquests reported in the *Morning Advertiser* of 5 May 1834 is particularly revealing:

> On Saturday, an Inquest was held before W. Baker Esq., Coroner at the Town of Ramsgate public house, Wapping Old Stairs, on the body of John Collett, an old fisherman, who had lived with his two daughters for the last twelve years in a small hatch-boat on the Thames. The inquiry created very great interest, in consequence of a report which had been promulgated that the deceased had died for want of the common necessaries of life, and that the parish had refused to relieve him. After hearing several witnesses, the Jury said it was plain enough that the old man had died for want of the common necessaries of life.

Four years later, the Poor Laws Commissioners published a report by Dr Thomas Southwood Smith mentioning Church Street in Bethnal Green (then a main thoroughfare) as needing a regular mud-cart to carry away the surplus mud and 'putrefying matter' and even Charles Dickens (in *Sketches by Boz*) drew attention to Ratcliff Highway as a 'reservoir of dirt, drunkenness and drabs'.

With so much of the local income dependent on the river, and the weather, bad winters in the 1850s and 1860s meant that families with no income were desperate enough to attack bakers' shops and anywhere that sold food, with the resultant poverty resulting in a string of bread riots in the East End. Starving labourers were even desperate enough to steal from their compatriots in the local workhouse, as a report in the *East London Observer* of 19 January 1861 reveals: 'A large body of labourers forcibly seized upon a quantity of bread as it was being delivered by the bread contractor at the door of Whitechapel workhouse', with one man seriously injured, striking 'terror' into the local tradesmen.

GETTING ABOUT

The coming of the railway can be said to have prompted the most rapid change – so far – to the appearance of the East End and the lifestyle of its residents.

The London and Blackwall Railway opened, linking Blackwall to the Minories in Aldgate, in 1840 (Fenchurch Street became the new terminus a year later). It also had a branch line to the Isle of Dogs, connecting the docklands, its infrastructure now part of the Docklands Light Railway. The original carriages were pulled along by cables, hence Cable Street, which links Whitechapel to Shadwell. Just three years later, the Brunels' Thames Tunnel (the first tunnel under a navigable river) opened as a foot tunnel for pedestrians but was not popular and was sold to the East London Railway in 1865, originally running trains to Brighton but now part of the East London tube line. Steam trains used the Thames Tunnel from 1869, and the line extended to Bow and to Millwall in 1871.

Additionally, the Eastern Counties Railway opened a line from Mile End to Romford in 1839. The North London Railway also operated a service through North London to Bow, and all these organisations (L&BR, ECR, NLR) were slowly linked and extended, although many of the stations (e.g. Victoria Park and St Mary's at Whitechapel) have since closed.

While the age of the train was having an impact on the area (displacing many during its construction, with the soot left behind by steam trains persuading others to move), horse-drawn trams were still in operation in the East End until 1900. The Thames was also important for passenger traffic until the middle of the nineteenth century, with watermen, and some long-standing ferry and steamer services, taking people from the East End to south London and beyond. To encourage workers to use the trains, the government offered cheap workmen's fares, but the displaced usually moved to different areas and had no use for the offer. What the railways did do, however, was speed up journey times.

Significantly, East Enders could also reach the seaside relatively easily from 1856 when the London, Tilbury and Southend Railway reached the coast. Those who could afford the fares, and who had previously taken day trips as far as, say, Epping Forest, could now travel further in a much shorter time (Southend had only been accessible by horse-drawn coach or steamer until then). Twenty years later, tens of thousands of East Londoners used the train to get to Kent or Sussex for two weeks' annual hop-picking, viewed as a holiday with pay then and well into the twentieth century.

The railway became even more popular than the river for day-trippers after the 1878 disaster when the *Princess Alice* paddle-steamer collided with a collier that had just left Millwall – the worst ever disaster on a British waterway, resulting in over 600 deaths.

To cope with the increasing road traffic – the horse and cart still playing a major role, of course – the Blackwall Tunnel, designed by Marc Isambard Brunel, was built to link Poplar to Greenwich on the other side of the Thames. It was opened fully in 1897 and was then the longest underwater tunnel in the world, at 6,200ft.

Entrance to Blackwall Tunnel.
Author's postcard collection

THE INDUSTRIAL REVOLUTION

In addition to the impact of the railways, the Industrial Revolution escalated the number of industries operating in the East End, and meant increased employment opportunities. While some local industries, such as weaving, struggled, other local factories were doing well – including Allen and Hanbury (pharmaceuticals) in Three Colts Lane, Bethnal Green, which had started out in the eighteenth century and continued to expand throughout the nineteenth; Batgers (confectionery) in Ratcliff; E. Moses and Son (clothing – said to supply the deposed king of France) in Aldgate; John Knight (soap-maker) in Wapping; and George Spill and Co. (who supplied 50,000 waterproof suits for the Crimea) in Stepney. Edward Cook's soap factory had moved from Whitechapel to a larger factory in Bow in 1859, known as the Soapery, and Maconochie's opened their factory for processed food in Limehouse in 1897, specialising in pickles.

Dogs were also catered for, with Spratts, the world's largest dog biscuit factory, opening just a few miles away in 1899.

Cigar and cigarette makers were doing well, with Godfrey Phillips (founded in 1844) employing 3,000 workers (over two-thirds of them women) in Commercial Street, Stepney, and Freemans in Shoreditch opening a second factory – in Cardiff – by the end of the nineteenth century. The tobacco industry was the biggest employer of Jewish immigrants in the 1860s in the East End until the Polish and Eastern European Jews arrived to work in the rag trade. The Zeegen family, Dutch Jews, were established cigar-makers in Chicksand Street, Spitalfields, by 1880. Bow's china industry was thriving, bearing in mind that there were more tidal mills on the River Lea than anywhere in the world, plus windmills.

Additionally, brick-making, shoe-making, paper-making, glass-making, brush-making, cabinet-making, chair-making, metalworking and upholstery manufacture proliferated in and around Bethnal Green in the nineteenth century. The everyday requirements of the worker were all being produced in the East End, together with some more exotic successes such as Jamrach's on Ratcliff Highway from 1840, famous for supplying exotic wildlife (including tigers and rhinos) to zoos and circuses as well as exotic pets such as wombats and monkeys.

As factories and warehouses opened and flourished, one industry was in drastic decline locally by the end of the nineteenth century – that of prostitution, vice having originally been one of Victorian Britain's biggest industries. The well-heeled were moving out of Stepney and its surrounds, and the brothels moved to where they were, i.e. the more upmarket parts of London. Pubs like Paddy's Goose in Shadwell, which had a reputation for rough entertainment and friendly whores, were on their way out.

THE FIGHT FOR IMPROVED PAY AND WORKING CONDITIONS

Victorian trade unionism was mainly the preserve of skilled workers, so, although there was work to be had, the struggling working class of East London became reliant on strikes to improve their standard of living. The 1,400 'Match Girls' of Bryant and May went on strike in 1888 as a protest against the conditions of the factory in Fairfield Road, Bow. They were being paid 4*s* per week for fourteen-hour days, often reduced by arbitrary fines for talking or going to the toilet (!) while risking the disease known as 'phossy jaw' from the unhealthy phosphorus-ridden working conditions. The strike, publicised in *The Link* newspaper, resulted in improvements within weeks in both pay and conditions for the girls.

A year later, gas workers in Canning Town achieved their aim of an eight-hour day following strike action, followed by garment workers and tailors. The latter featured in *The London Evening Standard* of 30 September 1889, with strikers described as 'malcontents' who 'consisted of East-end tailors, the undersized, ill-fed and ill-clothed German and Polish emigrants'. Some 1,000 tailors had assembled the day before at Buck's Row, Whitechapel, before marching to Hyde Park, although they had been on strike for several weeks by then, with one riot in Whitechapel mentioned in *St James's Gazette* on 5 September. Employers gave in, agreeing to a reduced (!) 12-hour day with refreshment breaks and no overnight 'home' work.

Even more crucially, more than 60,000 dock workers went on strike the same year to fight for the 'dockers' tanner' (6*d* an hour), a bitter and lingering battle that was also won, resulting in a strong trade union. This was a decade of strikes – which took place in other locations, of course, including neighbouring Becton (gas workers) and Silvertown (rubber factory workers) – proving the possibilities of improvement through united action; a watershed for the Labour movement.

HOW THE OTHER 'ARF LIVE

The Great Exhibition of 1851 showed the evolving disparity between the East End and the West End, rich and poor. There was a contemporary ballad called 'I'm going to See the Exhibition for a Shilling', which suggests that a costermonger or housemaid would need to pawn 'coat and trousers' to pay the entrance fee to view a 'shining diamond, worth seventy million pounds'. Exactly.

Perhaps on a par with modern-day fans of horror were the expensively garbed residents of Kensington and Mayfair who would travel by omnibus or hansom cab on excursions that historian Dr Matthew Green describes as 'poverty porn' in *London, A Travel Guide*, where they felt 'the attraction of repulsion' at the sight of the ragamuffins and the slums. This did have one positive outcome, however, with some stepping forward to actually do something about it.

PHILANTHROPY

This was to some extent the saviour of the Victorian East End. The individuals I list below all deserve detailed biographies (and some are out there), so, although their input was considerable, they are afforded little more than a cursory glance – with apologies:

Rev. Samuel, vicar of St Jude's, Whitechapel, and **Henrietta Barnett**: founded Toynbee Hall in 1884, the first 'university' settlement which aimed to bring the elite into the area to work with and educate the local community. The couple also set up the Children's Country Holiday Fund.

Dr Thomas Barnardo, studied at the London Hospital: founded the East End Juvenile Mission, which grew dramatically into the widespread Barnardo Homes organisation, and initiated the first Ragged School in Stepney (free education for the destitute). He also became involved in the emigration of destitute children, with, for example, 150 girls from the Stepney home embarking on a new life in Canada in July 1884, joining thousands of other migrants.

William Booth, Methodist preacher: although he began the East London Christian Mission in Whitechapel

in 1870 – which became the Salvation Army's headquarters – he had been preaching in a tent on the site of an old Quaker burial ground (which became the Blind Beggar public house) from 1865. Other accounts of the massive amount of charitable work he did locally are given in his 1867 report, which gives a taste of his outstanding philanthropy: soup kitchens, prayer meetings, poor relief, the introduction of a reading room, Bible classes and more.

Statue of William Booth in Mile End Road. *Author's collection*

Baroness Angela Burdett-Coutts, richer even than the queen in 1837: set up a sewing school in Spitalfields, a night school for youths in Shoreditch, the East End Weavers' Association, Columbia Market (a failed attempt to provide East Enders with cheap food), as well as helping initiate the NSPCC and the RSPCA and providing funds for the Ragged Schools movement. The East End is in her debt.

Frederick Charrington, brewer's son from Bow: renounced the demon drink (and an inherited fortune), and in 1886 initiated the largest prayer hall in Europe: the Great Assembly Hall in Mile End Road which held 5,000 people. He also spearheaded a national campaign against sexual immorality (responsible for closing down 200 backstreet brothels).

Rev. Osborne Jay, vicar of Holy Trinity, Shoreditch: began services in 1886 in a hayloft above stables with a congregation of fourteen, but increased attendance by providing a working men's club and gymnasium with a boxing ring. Amazingly, he raised £5,000 in one year for a 'proper' church – well over £500,000 today.

George Peabody, American businessman: built the first Peabody Building in Commercial Street, Spitalfields, in 1864, with four more blocks in Shadwell by 1867. These provided three-room flats for 5s a week (though this was still sadly beyond many of the local poor) and donated some £500,000 for similar buildings all over London.

Earl of Shaftesbury: patron of the Ragged Schools from 1884 (London's largest was in Copperfield Road, Mile End, now a museum), and reformed working conditions in mines and factories for young children in the East End and beyond (e.g. The Factory Act, Coal Mine Act).

Peter Bedford, Quaker silk weaver from Spitalfields: formed the Society for Lessening the Causes of Juvenile Delinquency, which, in 1867, combined with two other Quaker organisations for the local destitute, known as the Bedford Institute Association, helping with food poverty and funding for funerals etc. In 1893, William Palmer of Huntley and Palmer biscuits, another Quaker, left Hoxton Hall (which had housed the Blue Gospel Temperance Mission) to the BIA in his will.

Beatrice Potter-Webb and **Eleanor Marx** were what were called 'slummers', being just two of the women from middle- and upper-class backgrounds who immersed themselves physically in the lives of struggling Victorian East Enders using their influence and contacts to press for improved conditions.

THE START OF SLUM CLEARANCE

The *Illustrated London News* of 24 October 1863 drew attention to the plight of the poor in the Nichol in Shoreditch (and elsewhere in the East End) by referring to an inquest on a local child with death caused by 'blood-poisoning through the impure state of the dwellings', i.e. the 'extreme squalor'. The article gives profuse detail of the Nichol as 'reeking with disease and death ... filth and poverty,' the residents 'earning just enough to keep them from absolute starvation', many in the local sweatshops or working at home, making shoes or even smoking fish.

There had been many protests about landlords taking advantage of the shortage of what is now called affordable housing, not bothering with any form of maintenance, and ignoring the gross conditions – some of these took the form of rallies in Victoria Park – but to no avail.

However, the newly established London County Council was able to take advantage of the 1890 Housing for the Working Classes Act, giving them the power to demolish the slums. The Boundary Estate, with twenty-three blocks, replaced the slums, and incorporated a central garden and bandstand (Arnold Circus), shops and clean air, but lost its twelve public houses. The estate was formally opened on 3 March 1900 by the Prince and Princess of Wales, but was a social housing failure. Only eleven of the 5,719 evicted people moved back in, due to the high rents and the rules and regulations, so the dwellings were occupied by the employed and the lower middle classes, not the poverty-stricken. Already displaced by the railway development, these people moved into areas like Dalston and Walthamstow on the north London borders.

The Metropolitan Association for Improving the Dwellings of the Industrious Classes had already failed in 1849 with their first lodging house in Spitalfields (Spicer, now Buxton, Street). This 'Artisans' Home' had rooms for 234 single men over five floors, a worthy attempt at philanthropic housing, and the *Illustrated London News* of 19 January 1850 describes the spectacular coffee room with its cast-iron pillars, and points out the advantages of the gas lighting, the washrooms, toilets, reading room and kitchen available in the basement. This seems a bargain at just 3s per week, but nevertheless it was apparently perceived as too austere and uninviting (according to David Rich in *The Hamlets and The Tower*).

Baron Nathan Rothschild formed the Four Per Cent Industrial Dwellings Company in 1885 to provide cheap tenement dwellings for the influx of Jewish tenants (who had become more prevalent than the Huguenot weavers, the population of Spitalfields in 1901 being 95 per cent Jewish) in and around the notoriously deprived and vice-ridden Flower and Dean Street. The company was also intended to provide a reasonable return for its shareholders, and building was hastened by the Ripper murders in the area, the killings leading to public outrage and an interest in slum landlords and slum clearance. Such redevelopments were assisted by the 1868 Artisans and Labourers Act, which granted powers of slum clearance.

Earlier in the nineteenth century, the market gardens and grazing pasture adjacent to the East India Docks had been replaced by the development of Poplar New Town, and rural areas around Limehouse had been replaced by builders' rubble and housing. Cubitt Town (named after its developer) was built as a self-sufficient residential area on the Isle of Dogs with its own pubs, library, schools and place of worship.

DECLINE OF THE DOCKS

The Thames Ironworks had become one of the most important shipbuilders on the River Thames, and one of the biggest private shipbuilders in the country, launching, among many others, the first iron sea-going warship, HMS *Warrior*, in 1860. The *London* was also launched from Blackwall in 1864, foundering dramatically and famously two years later. Just as famous, the

Great Eastern had been built at nearby Millwall in 1858, designed by Isambard Kingdom Brunel and the largest vessel of its time.

Exports were climbing from the middle of the nineteenth century and imports were also on the increase – there were huge amounts of frozen meat arriving in Millwall dock from Australia in the 1880s, for example (one ship could carry 120 tons) and thousands of foreign cattle and sheep were arriving at Blackwall from Holland and Germany. Nevertheless, the docks were struggling to keep pace and were affected by over-optimistic ambitions, some particularly poor winters (e.g. 1866–7, which was accompanied by another cholera outbreak), changing patterns in international trade following the demise of the empire, and poor investment. Containerisation also had a huge impact because container ships needed less security and less hands-on handling, i.e. fewer workers, with the docks at Wapping not being big enough or deep enough to cope with their ever-expanding size. Both the mighty Thames Ironworks and the Millwall Ironworks and Shipbuilding Company were struggling by the end of the century, their struggles compounded dramatically by competition from expanding dockyards in the north. The end of the iron shipbuilding era came quickly, impacting dramatically on the local workforce.

Their in-house football clubs live on, however! West Ham FC originated as the (Thames) Ironworks in 1895, and Millwall FC was founded even earlier (1885) by workers of Morton's jam factory on the Isle of Dogs. Yarrow's at Blackwall hung on a bit longer by building launches, river steamers and even torpedo boats, but they too moved north (to the Clyde) at the beginning of the next century, citing high London wages as one reason.

NOT ALL GLOOM AND DOOM

The Whitechapel Baths and Wash House opened in 1847, offering a place to do the laundry as well as first- and second-class 'bathing'; first class meant an extra towel, more hot water and a nicer cubicle! Although they closed twelve years later, they reopened in 1878 and gradually added three swimming pools, a major perk for the locals. And culture was not ignored either with Bethnal Green Museum in Cambridge Heath Road (as it is now called) opening in 1872 and the Bethnal Green Free Library, London Street, opening four years later (public libraries opened in Whitechapel and Poplar twenty years later). The Whitechapel Art Gallery followed in 1901, and is still going strong.

Other facilities for enjoying leisure pursuits grew – there were thirty-two cricket pitches and thirty-seven tennis courts in Victoria Park by 1895, for instance. Poplar had its own bowling club and Blackwall its own rowing club by the mid-nineteenth century and what had become a dumping ground on the Isle of Dogs became a public park in 1895.

A Houndsditch businessman developed No. 20 Whitechapel Road in 1867 as the People's Market, a 'capacious galleried and tile-paved hall' (according to the *Survey of London*) which supplied cheap groceries, shoes, books and hot soup (300 gallons a day at 2*d* a portion) to the poverty-stricken locals. Also in Whitechapel, a coffee house called the Tee-to-tum is described in *The Daily Graphic* of 7 August 1890 as:

> An excellent institution which was established about three months ago, and is now in a flourishing state. It serves the purpose of people's refreshment room and recreation club. There is a reading room, where daily, weekly and foreign

papers may be perused, and the indulgements of billiards and bagatelle are also to be enjoyed as well as the delights of dominoes, chess and draughts.

A shame it's long gone!

Education, too, continued its advance following the Education Act of 1870, providing elementary education for all schoolchildren, although it was not yet free, so attendance records were slow to improve. Apart from schools opening for the local Jewish community, Catholic schools opened for the local Irish. Boys, of course, were given priority over girls, and Barnardo's new, large, home on Stepney Causeway from 1888 was not only home to 400 boys but provided schooling and industrial training in such skills as carpentry, tailoring, engineering, harness-making, bread-making and printing, not to mention offering facilities such as a library and swimming pool. The disabled were not forgotten, as there was a 'Cripples' Football Team' they could join.

The original printers at Dr Barnardo's Home in Stepney Causeway. *Author's postcard collection*

STAYING HEALTHY, IF NOT WEALTHY

Sir Joseph Bazalgette, an acclaimed engineer, sorted the poo problem in the East End and elsewhere in London with his sewer system completed in 1865, following the outcry over the Great Stink of 1858 when the weather was exceptionally hot and the foul River Thames was exceptionally smelly. His complex system of 1,300 miles of sewers under the London streets was the largest civil engineering project in the world at the time but he was dealing with the filthiest river in the world (the Thames). He avoided tunnelling under the centre of London, and his outfall sewers and pumping stations were located east of the River Lea, the sewage then discharged on the outgoing tide. Bazalgette was also one of the planners of the Blackwall Tunnel.

The health of East Enders, and the rest of London, improved once it was realised that dirty water – and not foul air – was mainly responsible for the devastating cholera epidemics. Following the death of over 5,000 people in 1866, a private enquiry confirmed that the East London Water Company had, in breach of its obligations, provided water for public use from the River Lea which was 'unfiltered' i.e. containing sewage and dead fish (although no one was prosecuted!). A new cholera dispensary had, coincidentally, recently opened in Bethnal Green, funded in part by the dowager Queen Adelaide (the wife of William IV, Victoria's uncle), and this developed into a general hospital by 1889.

Cholera precautions were considered, rightly, particularly important, and extended to raids of local markets by sanitary inspectors, who were looking out for such problems as rotten fruit being sold cheaply. *The Daily Graphic* of 1 September 1892 refers to one such raid in Wentworth Street resulting in 'a ton of rotten fruit being carried off. It was not so much on the stalls as under them that the inspectors directed their searching glances' with, for example, a basket of 'unsound' plums hidden under a neighbouring stall selling crockery.

The City of London Hospital for Diseases of the Chest opened in Bethnal Green in 1851, specialising in the treatment of tuberculosis, and the Poplar Hospital for Accidents in 1855. Additionally, the Dispensary for Women and Children was started in Virginia Road, Bethnal Green, in 1867 by two Quaker sisters (it later moved to Hackney Road and concentrated on children). The newly introduced usage of carbolic, hypodermics and chloroform were all saving lives at such local hospitals before the end of the nineteenth century. Those needing treatment (as outpatients) 'whose only recommendations are poverty, destitution and disease' had the Metropolitan Free Hospital in Carey Street, Stepney, founded by Joseph Cray, the son of campaigner Elizabeth Fry. This hospital moved to Spitalfields in 1875 and, after selling the site to the Eastern Railway Company a year later (to develop Liverpool Street Station) was able to open, with twelve beds specifically for the local Jewish community, in nearby Kingsland Road in 1885, lasting in various locations until 1977.

Another specialist site was the Albert Dock Hospital, established in 1890, the first branch hospital of the Seamen's Hospital Society caring for seamen as well as dock and riverside workers. Nine years later, the London School for Tropical Medicine was founded and attached to this hospital. Additionally, the East London Hospital for Children was established by a London Hospital doctor and his wife, a nurse, at Ratcliff Cross in 1868, using their own money. Sadly, Nathaniel Heckford, the doctor, died age 29 of tuberculosis in 1871, soon after Charles Dickens had visited the hospital. The author assisted with fundraising, enabling a move to a much larger building in Shadwell in 1877, opened by George III's granddaughter, the Duchess of Teck.

In the heart of the East End, Whitechapel's London Hospital was the first to introduce training for nurses – in 1895 – but had greater claims to fame, linked to early celebrity culture. In 1888, surgeon Dr Openshaw had been sent part of a kidney to examine, allegedly belonging to Catherine Eddowes, one of the Ripper's victims (identified in a letter from 'the Ripper' as a 'bit of innerds'). In 1890 Sir Frederick Treves at the London Hospital gave a home of sorts within the hospital to Joseph Merrick, the 'Elephant Man', to release him from the depravity of being part of a local freak show.

Those with mental health issues were not forgotten: while the Bethnal Green Asylum continued to expand, another institution opened in Bow in 1844: Grove Hall. This had started out as a pauper farm, until opening as a 'licensed house' (a private lunatic asylum) in 1844, with 400 inmates by 1849.

On a smaller scale Dr Thomas Allinson is worth a mention. He was a great proponent of the benefits of wholemeal bread, purchasing Bethnal Green Mill in 1892 so he could produce his own stone-ground wholemeal flour. The result was the Natural Food Company with a slogan of 'Health Without Medicine'.

SPARRERS CAN SING

The boom in music hall, locally and nationally, brought some welcome, if boisterous, entertainment to the East

End. It was certainly a great improvement on the sleazy side shows (the penny gaffs) and the type of freak shows that featured Joseph Merrick, although anyone wanting such downmarket entertainment still had McDonald's Music Hall in Hoxton featuring 'grotesques' and a 'mechanical donkey' in 1866. (It opened as Mortimer's Hall in 1863, and has had a varied life, surviving as a theatre to the current day, one of only two to do so locally.)

The New Royal Pavilion Theatre opened in 1827 in Whitechapel Road but burned down in 1856, its replacement in 1858 housing 3,700 (1,000 more than Covent Garden) with the largest pit in London theatre. Lusby's 'Summer and Winter Palace' in Mile End Road, dating from 1868 was another victim of fire (a common form of demise for theatres) but duly replaced by the Paragon Theatre in 1885, said to have staged the debut of Charlie Chaplin, and advertising itself in 1892 as 'the grandest place of amusement in Europe' and 'the best ventilated theatre in London'. Yet another theatre destroyed by fire (in 1896) was the Cambridge Music Hall in Commercial Street, Shoreditch, dating from 1864. It was rebuilt as the New Cambridge Music Hall in 1897, with another theatre close by from 1856 (the Shoreditch Empire, becoming the London Music Hall in 1895), also laying claim to an appearance by Charlie Chaplin. Shoreditch was spoilt for choice, with the National Standard Theatre in the High Street from 1837 (changing its name several times, again due to fire) offering opera and Shakespeare as an antidote to variety.

In Poplar there was the Queen's Palace of Varieties, which underwent a number of name changes from 1856, starting out as a room next to the Queen's Arms in Poplar High Street. Bow had the Eastern Empire from 1895, starting out as Bow Music Hall in Bow Road in 1855, but later becoming a cinema (in common with many variety theatres, of course). In Mile End was the People's Palace, opened by Queen Victoria in 1887 and offering rather more than just entertainment (in the Queen's Hall): it advertised itself as offering scientific and technical instruction and incorporated a swimming pool, gym and tennis courts. Over 900 students enrolled in its various evening classes in the first few months alone, signing up for diverse subjects such as languages, millinery or shorthand. Described variously as a 'Palace of Delights' and 'the University of the East End', it is now appropriately part of Queen Mary's College.

The most famous local music hall – and the other survivor – was built on the site of a pub by Mr Wilton in Wellclose Square in 1850. Opening as a music hall venue in 1859, it was renowned for its plush décor and huge central chandelier, and attempted to attract the respectable to a somewhat undesirable area. Early programmes feature opera and ballet as well as the ubiquitous burlesque, comic songs (e.g. Champagne Charlie) ... and trapeze. It had a struggle to achieve its aim, however, thanks to its location, and its fascinating history has at least one book all to itself.

Not everyone was a fan of music halls, of course. Take moral crusader Thomas Barnardo, for starters. He had erected a large mission tent in front of the Edinburgh Castle gin palace and music hall in Limehouse (in 1872) to try and convert its customers, and, having managed to raise enough money to buy the actual premises, converted it into a British Workman's Coffee Palace to replace what he regarded as the citadel of Satan. His alcohol-free bar was a success, with a reading room and library also available, and with part of the building operating as the People's Mission Church.

INCOMERS

In 1856, Prince Albert laid the foundation stone for the Stranger's Home for Asiatics, Africans and South Sea Islanders in West India Dock Road, offering comfortable and respectable lodgings, its name a sign of the times in Victorian East London. This was particularly welcomed by the Chinese, many of whom had arrived on ships with broken promises of return passage, and been abandoned (by the East India Company) in the area. The mid-1880s saw the development of Chinatown in and around Limehouse and Wapping, with Chinese grocery stores, eating houses, street names such as Canton Street and London's first Chinese laundry (in Poplar). Opium 'dens' opened, mainly to serve seamen who had become addicted on their travels, i.e. not just the Chinese, although for many Chinese opium smoking was a daily routine (and it was legal in Victorian London).

There was also an influx of Irish following the potato famine in Ireland between 1845 and 1850. Henry Mayhew wrote of his visit to the docks area in 1862 (*On The Waterfront*), referring to 'flaxen-haired sailors chattering in German' and 'a black seaman, with a red-cotton hand-kerchief twisted turban-like round his head'.

Additionally, the pogroms from 1881 after the assassination of the Tsar of Russia resulted in 200,000 Jewish inhabitants fleeing, with 30,000 settling in the East End. Yiddish became widely spoken in Whitechapel and Spitalfields, and the market in Middlesex Street (now Petticoat Lane) was dominated by Jewish traders specialising in second-hand clothing. Jewish immigrants from the Netherlands, known as chuts, settled around Spitalfields, specialising in cigar-making. One group of Orthodox Jews

Typical sight at Whitechapel Hay Market. *Motif collection*

took over a Huguenot church in Spitalfields in 1898, turning it into the Spitalfields Great Synagogue. In fact, by 1896 synagogues in and around Whitechapel alone were opened in New Road, Vine Court, Greenfield Street (now Greenfield Road), Great Alie Street, Scarborough Street, Mansell Street, Commercial Road and Plumber's Row. (See *Sketches of Christian Work and Workers* by Henry Walker, published by the Religious Tract Society 1896). The Jewish community took good care of its own during the latter part of Victoria's reign in particular, with Wellclose Square housing a Jewish almshouse and the Hand in Hand Home for Aged and Decayed Tradesmen, plus the Jewish Widows' Home Asylum in Great Prescot Street, and the Jewish Workhouse in Stepney Green. Such organisations were welcomed with open arms thanks to the often-foregrounded anti-Semitism, which blamed the Jews for everything from the sweatshops to overcrowding to the Ripper murders.

* * *

In the *Illustrated London News* of 19 March 1892, Clementina Black writes of the contrasting areas of the East End: 'Amid the ugliness lie delightful little nooks and corners.' She describes the smell of frying fish and of hay from the hay-carts in Whitechapel Road, and compares the 'discord' of the open-air stalls at Mile End Gate, with glimpses of 'squalor' among fine old houses. The East End was finding its identity – or, rather, identities.

9

THE 'MODERN' TWENTIETH CENTURY

Of necessity, this chapter is broken down into a near-breathless timeline, not only because of the increased rate of change (mainly for the good) in so many areas, but also because of the huge amount of documentation available for this period compared with previous centuries. So here we go. Hold on to your titfers …

1901 Whitechapel Art Gallery opened, designed by Arts and Crafts supremo William Morris.

1902 First meeting of the British Brothers' League (an anti-immigration organisation) at the People's Palace, Mile End, in front of 4,000 people.

1902 Stepney Green station opened.

1902 The Queen Victoria Seamen's Rest in Poplar formally opened by Princess Louise, offering free medical treatment and free banking.

1903 Lenin was the main speaker at the new Alexandra Hall in Jubilee Street, Stepney.

1903 Bow Road police station opened.

1903 Edith Cavell started work as assistant matron at the Shoreditch Infirmary, where she introduced a course in maternity nursing.

1903 The Workers' Educational Association launched at Toynbee Hall.

1904 This was the year when children born in the workhouse in St Leonard's Street, Bromley-by-Bow, started to have their birth place registered as 50A St Leonard's Street to avoid disadvantage in later life.

1904 The London County Council opened a new School of Engineering and Navigation at Poplar (Alfred Hitchcock studied there!).

1905 Wapping Fire Station opened on the corner of Red Lion Street.

1905 Grove Hall Asylum in Bow closed, with patients transferred to the Bethnal Green Asylum.

1906 Whitechapel Methodist Mission opened at Brunswick Hall in Whitechapel Road, providing food for poor children and a night shelter for homeless men.

1906 John Pounds Mission opened in Wellesley Street, Stepney to serve as 'the home of the cripple work in the East End' (*East London Observer*, 20 January 1906).

1907 The fifth Congress of the Russian Social Democratic Labour Party mobilised in Fulbourne Street, Whitechapel.

1907 Hill's in Shoreditch High Street, producers of cigars and cigarettes on a mammoth scale, won the contract to supply the Royal Navy with tobacco.

1907 The Fern Street Settlement founded for the local poor in Bromley-by-Bow by Clara Grant, a Wapping teacher. She introduced the 'farthing bundles', which were small parcels for children who were small enough to fit under a specially constructed arch.

1908 Stepney resident Clement Attlee switched from his Conservative stance to join the Limehouse branch of the independent Labour Party (Prime Minister 1945–51).

1909 The Reubens brothers, pimps from Rupert Street, Whitechapel, were executed for murder following an argument with a 'client' they were trying to rob.

1909 Walter Tull, brought up in a Bethnal Green orphanage, became Britain's first black professional outfield footballer when he was signed for Tottenham Hotspur, and later became the country's first black army officer (during the First World War).

1909 The United Horseshoe and Nail Company on the Isle of Dogs went into liquidation, mainly as a result of the arrival of the motor car.

1910 The Peabody Estate in Minerva Street, Bethnal Green, built, comprising 140 flats in seven blocks – with shared bathroom facilities.

1911 The Siege of Sidney Street, or the Battle of Stepney, a gunfight between Latvian revolutionaries (responsible for the death of three policemen during a jewellery heist in the City) and the police. The Latvians died when fire engulfed their hiding place.

1911 Thomas Cook featured an 'Evening Drive in the East End' for 5s. Their programme stressed the area's 'good policing' while mentioning 'vile alleys' and 'entirely unrelieved sordidness'! Tempting …

1911 The Jewish Maternity Home opened in Underwood Street, Whitechapel, complete with a midwifery training school.

1911 Albert Faccini started hiring out barrel organs from a depot in Ernest Road, Stepney, catering for those entertainers who could not afford to buy one.

1912 Feinman's Yiddish People's Theatre opened in Commercial Road with money raised from local immigrants – but only lasted six months due in part to arguments over opening on the Sabbath.

1912 The Lithuanian Roman Catholic Church of St Casimir opened in the Oval, Bethnal Green, indicative of the diverse ethnicity of the area.

1912 Bow Road police station opened.

1912 Imposing sculptures of dogs installed each side of the entrance to Victoria Park, courtesy of Lady Regnart – they were facsimiles of the Greek Dogs of Alcibiades.

Lithuanian RC church. *Dr Neil Clifton*

1913 Sylvia Pankhurst and other suffragettes attacked the Bow and Bromley Conservative Headquarters, breaking several windows, resulting in their being arrested and fined.

1913 Albert Stern House (originally Beth Holim) in Mile End Road opened as a hospital and old people's home for the local Spanish and Portuguese Jewish community (now owned by Queen Mary College and used as student accommodation).

1914 Anti-German riots in Poplar and Bethnal Green, with attacks on German-owned shops.

1914 300 women at Morton's canning factory in Millwall went on strike as a protest against low wages, achieving success after twelve days.

1914 Young pianist Solomon Cutner from Spitalfields made his debut at the Proms, aged 12.

1915 Issy Smith from Stepney became the first living recipient of the Victoria Cross for his bravery at Ypres.

1915 The Gunmakers' Arms public house, Old Ford Road, became the Mothers' Arms, a mother and baby clinic, thanks to the East London Federation of Suffragettes.

1916 HMS *Thunderer*, the last Royal Navy vessel to be constructed on the Thames at Blackwall, saw action at the Battle of Jutland.

1917 Upper North Street School, Poplar, bombed, killing eighteen children.

1917 The forerunner of the People's Dispensary for Sick Animals (PDSA) was opened in Whitechapel.

1918 Anti-war poet Isaac Rosenberg, a Stepney resident, killed in action.

1919 East End race riots against black seamen, with mobs of 4–5,000 attacking their lodging houses locally.

1919 Tubby Isaacs's jellied eel stall in Whitechapel opened on the site of an earlier snuff house.

1919 Jewish Hospital in Stepney Green completed.

1920 Bloom's Kosher Restaurant opened in Brick Lane, attracting such celebrities as Charlie Chaplin and the Marx Brothers.

1921 Thirty Poplar councillors jailed over a dispute between proposed increases in rates disproportionately affecting poorer boroughs, who would be charged the same fixed rate as the rich.

1921 The Rivoli Cinema, seating over 2,000, opened in Whitechapel on the site of a former music hall.

1922 Clement Attlee voted in as the Labour MP for Limehouse.

1922 George V opened Edward VII Memorial Park in Shadwell on the site of its short-lived fish market, which closed *c.* 1895.

1922 Billy 'Brilliant' Chang was the name of a leading opium dealer from Limehouse, arrested for supplying the drug to a showgirl who had died as a result (he was found not guilty).

1923 First annual ceremony of the Lilies and the Roses at the Tower of London in memory of the death of Henry VI (who died in 1471 while prisoner in the Tower).

1923 Children's House in Bow opened by H.G. Wells – a nursery on Montessori principles, instigated by pacifists Muriel and Doris Lester from Leytonstone.

1924 Harry Mallin from Shoreditch became the first Briton to successfully defend his Olympic gold middleweight boxing title (in Paris).

1925 MP for Mile End, John Scurr, drew attention in the House of Commons to the inconvenience of the hay and straw market, which disrupted Aldgate traffic.

1926 London Hospital, Whitechapel, had to close its outpatients department because of power cuts when workers at a local generating station joined the National Strike.

1926 Mary Hughes, the Quaker daughter of the author of *Tom Brown's Schooldays*, set up the Dew Drop Inn in Vallance Road in an old pub, and lived there until her death in 1941, discarding her privileged origins to focus on helping the needy.

1927 The Lenin Estate opened in Bethnal Green, slammed by the *Daily Mirror* as 'luxury flats for Socialists' in 'the very red borough of Bethnal Green'.

1927 Wickhams Department Store opened in Mile End Road.

1927 The East London Child Guidance Clinic opened at the Jewish Hospital on Stepney Green.

1928 A tidal surge caused devastating flooding on and around the Isle of Dogs, necessitating relocation for many.

1928 Kingsley Hall Community Centre opened in Bow, thanks to peace campaigners Muriel and Doris Lester.

1928 Queen Mary opened a grand £2 million extension at Spitalfields Market.

1928 The Whitechapel Hay Market came to an end.

1929 York Hall Baths opened in Bethnal Green Road: became famous as a boxing venue.

York Hall, Bethnal Green.
Tom Bastin, via Flickr

1929 The Youth Hostels Association was launched at Toynbee Hall.

1930 The first Asian grocery store in the UK (Taj Stores) opened in Brick Lane.

1931 Mahatma Gandhi stayed at Kingsley Hall, Bow, during a visit to the UK.

1931 Stepney's Miriam Moses became the first female mayor of Stepney, and the first Jewish female mayor in the country.

1931 Ted 'Kid' Lewis, the champion boxer from Aldgate, became the 'New Party' parliamentary candidate for Stepney at the general election, but all NP candidates were defeated.

1932 Toynbee Hall Musical Society formed for East End workers to study music and attend concerts at nominal fees.

1932 The Children's Hospital in Shadwell became the Princess Elizabeth of York Hospital for Children.

1932 Some 16,000 people turned out for the funeral procession of the flamboyant King of Limehouse, Charlie Brown, landlord of the Railway Tavern, which housed a host of curiosities donated by its sea-going customers.

1933 A fire at Poplar's Rum Quay, West India Docks, resulted in the loss of a million gallons of rum.

1933 The Victorian store-yard and headquarters of the Royal National Lifeboat Institution (RNLI) in Poplar closed when the charity moved to larger premises in Elstree.

1934 The first British Union of Fascists (BUF) branch in East London was established at Bow.

1934 The pea-souper fog of January meant that the Troxy Cinema in Commercial Road had to close because it had actually infiltrated the theatre.

1934 Originally a Victorian building, Poplar Baths was renovated and reopened in East India Dock Road, its grim exterior earning it the nickname of Poplar Gaol.

1934 East London College, based in what was the People's Palace, awarded a Royal Charter and relaunched as Queen Mary's College as 'East London College' was felt to be pejorative (!)

1934 The Pavilion Theatre in Whitechapel, home to Yiddish theatre, closed.

1935 The Council of Citizens of East London formed to combat anti-Semitism.

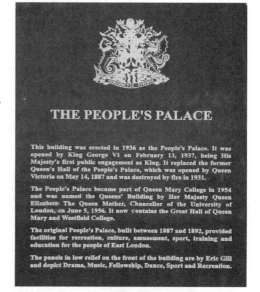

THE PEOPLE'S PALACE

This building was erected in 1936 as the People's Palace. It was opened by King George VI on February 13, 1937, being His Majesty's first public engagement as King. It replaced the former Queen's Hall of the People's Palace, which was opened by Queen Victoria on May 14, 1887 and was destroyed by fire in 1931.

The People's Palace became part of Queen Mary College in 1954 and was named the Queens' Building by Her Majesty Queen Elizabeth The Queen Mother, Chancellor of the University of London, on June 5, 1956. It now contains the Great Hall of Queen Mary and Westfield College.

The original People's Palace, built between 1887 and 1892, provided facilities for recreation, culture, amusement, sport, training and education for the people of East London.

The panels in low relief on the front of the building are by Eric Gill and depict Drama, Music, Fellowship, Dance, Sport and Recreation.

Plaque outside People's Palace. *Author's collection*

1936 The Battle of Cable Street: fascists vs non-fascists.

1936 A lido opened in Victoria Park catering for 1,000 bathers.

1936 The Council for the Promotion for Occupational Industries among the Physically Handicapped (CPOIPH) opened a centre for women in Upper North Street, Poplar, training physically handicapped women (in their hundreds) to weave rugs and embroider.

1937 Kelly's Pie and Mash shop opened in Roman Road, Bow.

1937 Communist and one-time suffragette Rose Cohen from Whitechapel executed in Moscow for espionage.

1938 St Mary's tube station in Whitechapel closed.

1938 Following the Munich crisis, sandbags appeared around the newly opened Poplar Town Hall.

1939 Picasso's Guernica on display at the Whitechapel Art Gallery in April.

1939 Aldgate jellied eel legend Tubby Isaacs and sons emigrated to the US to avoid war – but his sons enlisted when the US joined in.

1940 Docks at Limehouse and St Katharine bombed, and St Mary's Church, Whitechapel, destroyed: Stepney and Bethnal Green badly hit, the blitz continuing until 1941.

Heinkel over the Isle of Dogs, 1941. *Battlefield Historian*

1941 German spy Josef Jakobs was the last person to be executed at the Tower of London.

1942 The Princess Elizabeth of York Hospital for Children in Shadwell merged with the Queen's Hospital for Children in Bethnal Green and was renamed the Queen Elizabeth Hospital for Children.

1943 East India Dock at Blackwall became a construction site for the artificial Mulberry harbour used on D-Day.

Memorial of Bethnal Green disaster in Library Gardens. *Author's collection*

1943 The worst wartime civilian disaster took place at Bethnal Green tube station, when 174 people were killed in panic trying to find cover from what they mistakenly thought was an enemy attack.

1944 The first flying bomb, the V1, hit Grove Road, Mile End, killing six people.

1945 The last German V2 rocket to fall on London landed in Vallance Road, Bethnal Green, killing 130 people.

1945 Mile End returned Phil Piratin as the only communist MP for an English constituency.

1946 Wapping Group of Artists founded.

1946 Entertainers Elsie and Doris Waters from Bow awarded the OBE for their war work with the Entertainments National Service Association (ENSA).

Charrington's dray. *National Brewery Centre, Burton on Trent*

1946 The last brewery horse owned by Charrington's Brewery was sold when all their transport was mechanised.

1947 The Nag's Head Housing Estate was completed in Bethnal Green on the site of a pig farm.

1948 The London Hospital, Whitechapel, joined the new NHS.

1948 Royal Foundation of St Katharine moved to Butcher Row, Limehouse (which later became a hotel as well as a retreat centre).

1949 The Forester's Cinema in Cambridge Heath Road reopened after restoration following war damage.

1950 The first halal butcher in Britain opened in Hessel Street, Whitechapel.

1951 Lansbury Estate, Poplar, opened as part of the Festival of Britain (named after local politician George Lansbury, a Bow resident).

1952 A December pea-souper reduced visibility on the Isle of Dogs to zero and was recorded as one of the UK's worst air pollution disasters.

1953 Detectives drove around the streets of Stepney in April warning against handling rabbits stolen from Vallance Road, as they had been taken from a Venereal Disease Laboratory.

1954 The People's Palace in Mile End was sold to Queen Mary's College.

1955 Princess Margaret opened the new Church Community Centre of St Nicholas and All Hallows at East India Docks, Poplar.

1956 A ceremony took place at the Whitechapel Bell Foundry to cast and name the Big Bell of Bow (for St Mary Le Bow in the City: Cockneys are defined by being born within earshot).

1957 East Ender Bernard Kops found fame with his play *The Hamlet of Stepney Green* (and went on to become a very successful playwright).

1957 Victoria Park Station finally demolished after being closed for many years.

1958 The Jews' Free School moved out of Whitechapel (to Camden Town, a few miles north). It had sustained irreparable damage during the war, though the children, including those who had arrived via Kindertransport, had been safely evacuated.

1959 The German Roman Catholic Church of St Boniface built in Adler Street, Whitechapel (opened a year later, now Grade II listed).

1959 The Tower Hamlets Campaign for Nuclear Disarmament (THCND) started off as Stepney and Poplar Against the Bomb.

1959 In July, acting legend John Gielgud gave a gala preview of his one-man Shakespeare recital *Ages of Man* at St Margaret's House Community Centre in Bethnal Green in aid of Oxford House (a mini Oxford college for the poor just a mile away).

1960 This year's report from the Medical Officer of Health for Stepney confirmed 1,267 cases of tuberculosis and 360 cases of overcrowded residential 'facilities', among a whole raft of other rather depressing statistics.

1960 Poplar workhouse demolished.

1960 Barley Mow brewery, Limehouse, closed.

1961 On the day that betting shops became legal (1 May), Morgan's opened for business in Shoreditch.

1962 Stepney-born Lionel Bart's new play *Blitz* – about the East End during the war – opened at the Adelphi in London.

1963 The art deco Troxy in Commercial Road reopened after a three year closure, as the London Opera Centre.

1964 A ten-storey block of flats for the staff at London Hospital in Whitechapel opened, named after an eighteenth-century resident surgeon: John Harrison House.

1965 The London Borough of Tower Hamlets set up, incorporating Bethnal Green, Poplar and Stepney.

1966 Gangster George Cornell was famously shot by Ronnie Kray in the Blind Beggar, Whitechapel.

1966 Tower Hamlets Cemetery, full to the brim, closed for burials, but remained as parkland, nature reserve and woodland.

1967 East India Docks closed.

1967 The second Blackwall Tunnel opened parallel to the very busy first tunnel, easing congestion.

1967 The Naz, the first local cinema for the Asian community, opened in Brick Lane.

1968 St Katharine Docks and Wapping Docks followed in the footsteps of the East India Docks.

1969 The Krays were sentenced to life imprisonment for two murders, George Cornell and Jack 'the Hat' McVitie.

1969 Barnardo's moved out of its Stepney premises to Barkingside, Essex.

1969 Repton Boxing Club in Bethnal Green voted top amateur boxing club in London.

1970 More dock closures – West India and Millwall.

1970 The Isle of Dogs declared independence from the UK as a protest against the lack of local facilities, but did not receive enough support to achieve its aim.

1971 The police station in East India Dock Road closed and was subsequently demolished.

1971 800 pupils at Sir John Cass and Redcoat School in Stepney went on strike because their teacher, Chris Searle, had been fired for publishing a book of their poetry, using East End vernacular.

1971 The Globe Rope Works in Millwall closed.

1972 The Half Moon Theatre opened in Alie Street, Whitechapel, in a converted synagogue.

1972 Imposing Victorian store and landmark the Scotch House, Aldgate, destroyed by fire.

1972 London dockers strike again, this time against containerisation.

1973 The Tower Hotel, near to the Tower of London, opened as the third largest in London with 826 beds.

1973 York Square in Limehouse designated a conservation area; its public house, the Queen's Head, is said to have inspired the Queen Vic in *East Enders*.

1973 The 1920s Arts and Crafts community centre in Bow, Kingsley Hall, listed Grade II.

1974 An IRA bomb exploded at the Tower of London, injuring forty, one fatally.

1974 The Ten Bells public house in Fournier Street changed its name, controversially, to Jack the Ripper.

1975 Poplar Hospital closed.

1976 Following the closure of Charrington's Anchor Brewery in Mile End Road the year before, the building was finally demolished.

1976 Mala Sen and other activists created the Bengali Housing Action Group, challenging racism within the local council and successfully pressuring them to improve housing.

1976 The Jamme Masjid Mosque opened in Brick Lane, converted from an abandoned synagogue.

1977 St Katharine Docks reinvented as a yachting marina and opened by the queen.

1978 7,000 Asians joined a demonstration following the murder of Bangladeshi textile worker Altab Ali in Adler Street, Whitechapel. (Twenty years later, a park was renamed here in his memory.)

1979 Wapping Pierhead designated a conservation area.

1979 Bryant and May's match factory in Bow closed.

1980 South West India Docks closed.

1981 Cheryl Baker, from Bethnal Green, was one quarter of Buck's Fizz who won Eurovision with 'Making Your Mind Up'.

1982 Billingsgate Fish Market moved to the old West India Dock.

1983 Princes Street synagogue, Spitalfields, closed.

1983 The redevelopment of docklands began with the opening of an Enterprise Zone on the Isle of Dogs and a new road scheme opened by Princess Alexandra.

1983 Limehouse Studios opened in docklands, housing Channel 4.

1983 After nearly 200 years, the Bird Fair (later the dog market) in and around Club Row, Bethnal Green, finally gave in to legislation against selling live pets. No longer could traders sell yellow-painted sparrows from Hackney as canaries ...

1984 The Chaucer Theatre opened in Aldgate with a production from the Eastend Theatre Company: *A Day at the Opera, A Night at the Races.*

1985 The East London Mosque built in Whitechapel Road.

1985 Prince Charles visited Toynbee Hall during its centenary year.

1986 Rupert Murdoch's newspaper empire moved to Wapping.

1987 Docklands Light Railway (the DLR) opened by the queen.

1987 The Limehouse Paperboard Mills in Narrow Street, Limehouse, closed (but survived and expanded into Essex).

1988 'The Academy' opened in Whitechapel Road, offering drama tuition with performances in its own theatre, but caused controversy with its musical version of *Jack the Ripper.*

1989 The Truman Brewery in Brick Lane closed.

Docklands Light Railway. *Dr Neil Clifton*

1989 The London Arena opened in Millwall, seating 12,000 for concerts or ice hockey.

1990 The Ragged School Museum opened in Copperfield Road, Mile End.

1990 The London Hospital, Whitechapel, granted Royal title.

1991 The tallest building in Britain opened in the Canary Wharf development: No. 1 Canada Square.

1991 George Carey from Bow became Archbishop of Canterbury.

1991 The fruit and vegetable market at Spitalfields moved to Leyton, further east, but the market continues to thrive with a focus on boutiques, antiques and eateries.

1992 Brick Lane Music Hall opened, on the site of Truman's closed brewery.

1993 Keeling House in Bethnal Green, a sixteen-storey building, became the first post-war tower block to be listed.

1993 Opening of the Limehouse Link, Britain's most expensive stretch of road.

1994 40,000 people marched through Tower Hamlets in a Unite Against Racism demonstration, ousting the British National Party's councillor (Derek Beackon) from his short-lived victory the year before on the Isle of Dogs.

1995 Ronnie Kray's funeral, accompanied by a rendition of the popular 'My Way', held at St Matthew's in Bethnal Green, with mobs unable to get in.

1996 Blooms's kosher restaurant in Aldgate closed.

1996 The IRA set off a bomb on the Isle of Dogs, killing two and injuring more than 100.

1997 Marco Pierre White opened Café Pelican in Canary Wharf.

1998 The ward of Spitalfields renamed 'Spitalfields and Banglatown'.

1999 The first retail outlet opened in the financial centre at Canary Wharf: Boots.

1999 One of several London nail bomb attacks took place in Brick Lane, injuring five, generated by a lone neo-Nazi.

1999 The police station in Arbour Square, Stepney, which once held the Krays, closed (it is now flats).

1999 Barbara Windsor opened the new Genesis cinema in Mile End Road.

* * *

As Barbara herself might have said, Fings Ain't What They Used To Be. Something certainly true of the East End, which continues to cope with the pace of change in its people and its buildings into the twenty-first century.

SELECT BIBLIOGRAPHY

Barton Baker, H., *History of the London Stage and Its Famous Players (1576–1903)* (London: Geo. Routledge & Sons, 1904)

Besant, Sir Walter, *Early London* (London: A&C Black, 1908)

Bird, Samantha L., *Bloody British History – East End* (Stroud: The History Press, 2013)

Cox, Jane, *London's East End* (London: Weidenfeld and Nicolson, 1994)

Cox, Jane, *Old East Enders* (Stroud: The History Press, 2013)

Cruikshank, Dan, *Spitalfields* (London: Windmill Books, 2017)

Defoe, Daniel, *A Journal of the Plague Year* (London: E. Nutt, 1722)

Finch, Harold, *The Tower Hamlets Connection* (London: Tower Hamlets Library Services, 1996)

Gairdner, James (ed.) 'Gregory's Chronicle: 1435–1450' in *The Historical Collections of a Citizen of London in the Fifteenth Century* (London: Camden Society, 1876)

Glinert, Ed, *East End Chronicles* (London: Allen Lane, 2005)

Gordon, Dee, *The Little Book of the East End* (Stroud: The History Press, 2010)

Green, Matthew, *London, A Travel Guide Through Time* (London: Michael Joseph, 2015)

Greenwood, Pamela, Dominic Perring and Peter Rowsome, *From Ice Age to Essex* (London: Museum of London Archaeology Service, 2006)

Hall, Jenny and Ralph Merrifield, *Roman London* (London: HMSO, 1986)

Howse, Geoffrey, *Foul Deeds and Suspicious Deaths in London's East End* (Barnsley: Wharncliffe Books, 2005)

Kerrigan, Colm, *A History of Tower Hamlets* (London: London Borough of Tower Hamlets, 1982)

Linnane, Fergus, *London The Wicked City* (London: Robson Books, 2007)

Long, David, *Bizarre London* (London: Constable and Robinson, 2013)

Marcan, Peter, *An East London Album* (Peter Marcan Publications, 1992)

Marriott, John, *Beyond the Tower* (London: Yale University Press, 2011)

Marshall, Geoff, *London's Docklands* (Stroud: The History Press, 2018)

McDonnell, Kevin, *Medieval London Suburbs* (Chichester: Phillimore & Co., 1978)

Morrison, Arthur, *Tales of Mean Streets* (London: Methuen, 1894)

Oxford Dictionary of National Biography

Palmer, Alan, *The East End* (London: John Murray, 1989)

Parnell, Geoffrey, *The Tower of London* (London: B.T. Batsford, 1993)

Pepys, Samuel, *Diary 1659–1669* (First published 1825)

Rich, David, *The Hamlets and The Tower* (London: Tower Hamlets Local History Library, 2000)

Rule, Fiona, *London's Docklands* (Surrey: Ian Allan Publishing, 2009)

Smith, Stephen, *Underground London* (London: Little, Brown, 2004)

Stafford, Elizabeth, *Landscape and Pre-History of the East London Wetlands* (Oxford: Oxford Archaeology Ltd, 2012)

Stone, Peter, *The History of the Port of London* (Barnsley: Pen and Sword, 2017)

Stow, John, *Survay* [*sic*] *of London* (Originally published 1598)

Tames, Richard, *East End Past* (London: Historical Publications, 2004)

Tames, Richard, *London* (Oxford: Signal Books, 2006)

Taylor, Rosemary and Christopher Lloyd, *A Century of The East End* (Stroud: Sutton Publishing, 1999)

Thomas, Chris, *Life and Death in London's East End* (London: Museum of London Archaeological Service, 2004)

Webb, Simon, *Unearthing London* (Stroud: The History Press, 2011)

Weightman, Gavin, *London's Thames* (London: John Murray Publishers, 2004)

Wise, Sarah, *The Blackest Streets* (London: Vintage Books, 2009)

DOCUMENTED SOURCES AT TOWER HAMLETS LOCAL HISTORY ARCHIVE

Anthony, Sian and Steve Ford, *Excavation of an Early Roman Occupation Site and Prehistoric Finds at Express Wharf, Isle of Dogs* (Archaeology Data Service, 2001)

Coles, Sarah, Steve Ford and Andy Taylor, *White Swan Public House, Yabsley Street, Blackwall Post Excavation Assessment Report* 02/54C (Reading: Thames Valley Archaeological Services Ltd, 2003)

Smith, Reginald, 'Remains of Roman burials' in *Proceedings of the Society of Antiquaries*, June 1910

ADDITIONAL DOCUMENTATION

Cass, Simon and Steve Preston, *Roman and Saxon Burials at Steward Street, Tower Hamlets*, published by London and Middlesex Archaeological Society, 2009

The three voyages of Martin Frobisher, in search of a passage to Cathaia and India by the North-west, A.D. 1576–8. Reprinted from the first ed. of *Hakluyt's Voyages*, with selections from manuscript documents in the British Museum and State Paper Office. By Rear-Admiral Richard Collinson, 1867.

Guildhall Library Manuscripts Section: parish register entries, part of the Black and Asian Londoners in the City project, 2009.

SOME USEFUL WEBSITES

archaeology.co.uk
britannica.com
british-history.ac.uk
britishnewspaperarchive.co.uk
crossrail.co.uk
derelictlondon.com
elizabethan-era.org.uk
exploringeastlondon.co.uk
footprintsoflondon.com
hidden-london.com
historic-uk.com
london.anglican.org
londonslostrivers.com
lostcityoflondon.co.uk
mernick.org.uk
millsarchive.org
nationalarchive.gov
normanconnections.com
oldbaileyonline.org
pla.co.uk (Port of London Authority)
spitalfieldslife.com
the-east-end.co.uk
thehistoryoflondon.co.uk
towerhamlets.gov.uk
victorian-era.org
whitechapelsociety.com

INDEX